Exeter

Exeter

HISTORICALLY SPEAKING

BARBARA RIMKUNAS

This book belongs to:

Al Acampora

2010

Charleston | London

THE
History
PRESS

Published by The History Press
Charleston, SC 29403
www.historypress.net

Cover design by Natasha Momberger

First published 2008

Manufactured in the United States

ISBN 978.1.59629.486.8

Library of Congress Cataloging-in-Publication Data

Rimkunas, Barbara.
Exeter : historically speaking / Barbara Rimkunas.
p. cm.
ISBN 978-1-59629-486-8
1. Exeter (N.H. : Town)--History--Anecdotes. 2. Exeter (N.H. : Town)--Biography-
-Anecdotes. 3.   Exeter (N.H.)--History--Anecdotes. 4.   Exeter (N.H.)--Biography--
Anecdotes. I. Title.
F44.E9R56 2008
974.2'6--dc22
                            2008031396

CONTENTS

CONTENTS

INTRODUCTION

The *Exeter News-Letter* has been published in Exeter, New Hampshire, continuously since 1831. Throughout its long history, even as it evolved from an agricultural to a local newspaper, there was room for retrospection. Local historians, both amateur and professional, contributed historical stories, anecdotes and tales. Even if they were occasionally guilty of perpetuating a few urban legends, if anything can be said of Exeter and its environs it is that we are well aware of our history.

Some towns are quite silent with respect to their history, but Exeter is an old town (founded in 1638) and we are indebted to those writers—Benjamin Swasey, Roland Sawyer, Ernest Templeton, Olive Tardiff and Nancy Merrill—who kept us continually informed about our past.

When Nancy Merrill became director of collections at the Exeter Historical Society in the 1970s, she became the *Exeter News-Letter's* new history writer. Nancy was always interested in places and wrote more about the geography of the town than had previous chroniclers. Her meticulous research made her the obvious choice to write the town's official history book in 1988. *Exeter, New Hampshire: 1888–1988*, published to coincide with the town's 350th birthday, was so popular that the *News-Letter* was able to drop the history column for a number of years.

When I arrived at the Exeter Historical Society in 2000, fresh off a high school teaching career, Nancy Merrill, now happily retired, was still volunteering there. Before her encyclopedic memory began to drift away, Nancy would walk me through the archives, chuckling fondly, telling stories of Exeter's past. "You know," she might say, "the old courthouse burned right after an exhibit of 'The Burning of Moscow' played there." It would take me years to track down the historical evidence for many of these memories, but Nancy was usually right. I'd find it, one day, in a folder marked with Nancy's handwriting.

INTRODUCTION

The Exeter Historical Society, like any local historical society, is a beehive of activity. People of all ages find their way to our doors in search of the past. Children want to hear about fire engines and trains. Adults wonder why they keep finding so many rusty old nails in the garden and why their street is called "Tan Lane." Who was Lewis Cass? How come the ball field is called "Brickyard Park"? Why are there so many people in town named "Gilman"? These are the everyday questions posed to the staff and volunteers of the Exeter Historical Society.

In 2004, Editor Deb McDermott decided it was time to put history back into the *Exeter News-Letter*. Would I, the new curator, be willing to take on the task? Sure, why not? My early college term papers were criticized for having a "light, breezy" style of prose that I later transformed into the deathly arid tone preferred by academics. With a broader audience, I was free to write history that someone might actually want to read. WWND? What Would Nancy Do? Nancy, if given the chance, would walk everyone through the narrow shelves of the Exeter Historical Society archives, casually telling the history of the town. There are a million stories in there, and I owe it to her to set them free.

EXETER'S WORKING WATERFRONT

It is possible today to walk along the shops on Water Street in Exeter and not notice the river flowing behind the buildings. The various shops and offices are designed to face the street to lure in customers and the river serves mostly as a boundary line. But for nearly three centuries, the river was the focal point of town and the lifeline between Exeter and the outside world.

Europeans would never have settled on this plot of land if it hadn't been for the waterfalls and the two rivers that make up the Exeter-Squamscott system. The freshwater Exeter River, flowing over the rocks in the central part of town into the brackish tidal Squamscott River, created the power source they needed to run their many mills. The Squamscott was the egress to the outside world. Quickly using the landscape's dense forests for lumbering and shipbuilding, they stripped the resources by the beginning of the nineteenth century. By then, the river had become invaluable for shipping goods into and out of town.

Once Exeter's lumber was gone, the river was needed to bring firewood into town. New industries, such as paper, leather and printing, developed in Exeter and goods were also shipped out of town. By 1827, when the Exeter Manufacturing Company was created, there were well-established shipping lines to tap for bringing in raw cotton and sending out cotton cloth. Not that this was always easy—an oxbow, a sharp twist in the river located just below Route 101—made navigating the Squamscott difficult. Most schooners found that it was necessary to get a tow into town.

If you could travel back in time, you would find that most of the heavy work in town was happening behind the Water Street shops. Goods were brought up the Squamscott via Portsmouth and unloaded in the rear in much the same way supermarkets are supplied by trucks today. This bustle of activity was described by Dr. William Perry: "The clerks were kept busy,

A schooner at the wharf in Exeter, circa 1880.

shoveling and measuring the corn and salt, which were brought in bulk by water, and dumped on the lower floors of the stores opening toward the river." Nonperishable goods were shipped less frequently. "The merchants went to Boston in the spring and fall and brought goods to last them through the following months. They spent two or three days in selecting their stock, shipping it to Portsmouth to be reloaded on Captan Furnald's packet for Exeter. Quite a little time it took to get the goods here, and a lively day it was, and very interesting for us boys, when the packet discharged her cargo." Captain Furnald ran a regular service between Portsmouth and Exeter with his sturdy gundalows.

Outlaying towns transported most of their shippable goods in winter when freezing temperatures would prevent spoilage. Dr. Perry noted: "In winter days you could see on Water Street a long row of pungs from far back in the state, loaded with butter and dried apples and carcasses of mutton, which were exchanged for salt, southern corn and fish. Fresh fish was carried away frozen and the drivers of the pungs fed chiefly, during their journey, on chunks cut from frozen masses of baked beans."

Exeter's waterfront around 1870. Rough-looking wharves and warehouses indicate a thriving river economy. Although the railroad was beginning to take over transportation of manufactured goods, the river was still considered the best way to move heavy and bulky goods such as coal and lumber.

Merchants found a ready market in town for goods that could not be produced locally. Rum, sugar and molasses were shipped in from the West Indies. Whale oil, for lighting, was hauled in by the cask, and Perry remembers flour shipped in from Baltimore.

By the mid-nineteenth century, the railroad had arrived and many merchants took advantage of its cheaper and more dependable service. A channel was cut across the oxbow in the 1880s to ease the navigation difficulties, but the days of water transport were numbered. Silting issues, combined with the bridges built downriver made it difficult to slip in with the tide. Barges came up the river with bricks, wood and coal into the 1930s, but by World War II there was no longer a need for a working waterfront in Exeter.

THE PISCATAQUA
GUNDALOW

Before there were trucks and adequate highways, Exeter was a seaport by necessity. The Squamscott River provided the only reliable transportation network available, but it had some severe limitations. Originating on Great Bay, the Squamscott's waters, like all the rivers in the Piscataqua estuary, ebb and flow with the tide. Combine this with its treacherous currents —described as "cross-grained and wily waters" by the late William Saltonstall, former principal of Phillips Exeter Academy and local historian—and one can easily imagine the difficulties involved in shipping goods up or down the river.

To tame the rivers of the Piscataqua region, a new type of vessel was required. It needed to be rugged, maneuverable and low-keeled. It had to haul heavy loads without overturning and it had to handle the shallow waters of low tide. By the colonial period, movement in the Piscataqua region was dominated by the packet—a small, sturdy vessel powered by wind and tide. It was excellent for transporting people, but the keel was too deep for heavy loads and shallow water. Shipwrights began to create a flat-bottomed barge suitable for transporting large loads of lumber. By the early 1800s, the design had been perfected to meet the needs of the region with a spoon-shaped bow and elegantly rounded stern. A lateen sail was added to take advantage of wind power. This sail, on a short mast, could be lowered to pass under a bridge. A rudder and leeboard provided the maneuverability required to glide into and out of deep currents.

The gundalows were never meant to be used on the open sea, although there are a few accounts of trips made to Boston. Their job was primarily to shuttle goods between the port of Portsmouth and the inward towns of Exeter, Dover, Berwick and Newmarket. Although similar craft were found in Maine, the triangular sail marks the Piscataqua gundalow as a vessel

A typical Piscataqua gundalow, heavily loaded with wood.

unique to the region. The fact that they traveled with the tides is clear in the ledger of Joseph Fernald, an Exeter shipper who operated several gundalows from a wharf once located on the current site of Swasey Parkway. Fernald charged Exeter businessmen for "freighting" and noted in the ledger the goods going "down" river to Portsmouth or "up" river to Exeter.

Captain Fernald's busy gundalows hauled lumber, paper, furniture and leather goods to Portsmouth on the ebb tide and returned later on the rising tide with molasses, lime, fish, candles and rum—lots of rum. Exeter was a thirsty place before the temperance movement got going. The flat-bottomed gundalows could strand on the mud flats and wait out the tide if necessary (not a particularly fun experience if you're unprepared). Gundalow crews were scorned by other seamen as the lowest of their profession and schooner captain Johnson Stevens of Kennebunk was once quoted as saying, "A man

Gundalows were the workhorses of water transportation, carrying heavy loads of lumber, hay, bricks and other goods between the ports of Exeter and Portsmouth.

that would sail a Gundilo would rob the church yard." Perhaps all that rum was too much of a temptation when stranded on the mud flats.

Notwithstanding the good Captain's comments, the gundalow's crews were really able seamen considering the difficulties they encountered on their hauls. Gundalow traffic began to falter when steam-powered vessels began to move barges up the rivers. By the turn of the twentieth century, gundalow traffic had all but ended on the Squamscott River.

EXETER'S RIVER RATS

It is entirely fitting that the current Phillips Exeter Academy rowing team calls itself the "River Rats." They're probably not even aware that the name has a long tradition on the Squamscott River that dates back to the first part of the twentieth century. It takes someone with a long memory to recall the stories of the original River Rats.

Olive Tardiff, an Exeter native and author of *Exeter Squamscott: River of Many Uses*, recalled interviewing some of the River Rats while researching her book back in 1986. Remembering their boyhoods in the 1920s, Bill Damsell and Francis Bergeron (Exeter High class of '32), focused on the importance of the Squamscott River on their childhoods. Boys back then didn't have play dates set up by parents or enrichment activities or even organized sports. They had to invent their own fun, and by today's standards most of it was dangerous, irresponsible and quite possibly illegal. Living as they did near the river, the boys spent much of their free time in and around the Squamscott.

Walking along Swasey Parkway today, it is hard to imagine that it was not always the beautiful and scenic spot that it is now. For one thing, the town dump ran along the waterfront and all manner of vermin lived there. Most local boys owned a gun of some type and rats were fair and free game. No hunting season or license was needed. Everett Lamson, who lived on the upper end of Exeter River, recalled, "By the time an Exeter boy was thirteen years old, he was allowed to become the proud owner of a .22-caliber rifle, single shot and complete with instructions from his father about safety and aiming techniques." Safety wasn't usually a concern for most of the boys —they tried daredevil games such as shooting twigs out of one another's fingers—but the big sport was shooting rats down at the dump. "This was generally a night time sport," recalled Lamson, "since the rats came out in

Henry Shute and a friend take an afternoon walk and encounter one of the perils of summertime—skinny-dipping as a group of Exeter's river rats scurry for shelter.

droves at night to forage. A flashlight was held in the left hand beside the barrel of the .22-caliber rifle and sighted onto the rat. The animal had to be hit very accurately to drop him or he would just crawl off and die amongst the debris and boxes. The rats never seemed to grow to any giant sizes and perhaps our activity had something to do with it." When Swasey Parkway was created in the 1930s, the dump was moved to Court Street. Depression-era boys, brought up on the thrill of the hunt, took their girlfriends to the new dump for the excitement of rat hunting while on a date.

There was no town pool in Exeter in the 1920s and no air conditioning. Swimming was the favored way of cooling off during the long hot summer months. Girls usually didn't swim in the river because the preferred swimming attire was nothing at all, but boys saw no need to worry about such things with the cool waters of the Squamscott so near. It was worth the risk of getting caught in the altogether. But although the water may have been cool, it certainly wasn't clean. Generations of Exeter residents, under the impression that a tidal river will exchange water twice a day, had been dumping raw sewage and waste water directly into the river for several centuries. The problem had become acute by the late 1890s, but New England thriftiness had prevented the town from building adequate sewage systems. In 1933, the Committee for Improvement of Town Sewers reported:

> *A walk along Swasey Parkway would show even the casual observer the distressing, filthy, unsanitary, revolting spectacle. Where sight fails, the sense of smell reveals the condition. Sludge banks, that is, banks of settled solids of the sewage have been formed in front of each sewer outlet, and are easily visible above the water at low tide. At high tide they are evidenced by the belching of gasses from the covered sludge banks. To this situation are traceable many of the bad odors from the river, known to all of us. The river from Great Bridge to the middle of the Parkway is little more than a virtual cess pool.*

It was further noted that of eleven outlets located on the river, seven dumped raw sewage into the river. It is a testament to the River Rats' strong immune systems that any of them made it to adulthood, even though Olive recalls Francis Bergeron telling her that he would sometimes bob to the surface only to find toilet paper sticking to his head. And having experienced the ultimate "ick" factor, he continued, like most of the River Rats, to hang around his beloved Squamscott for years to come.

Was the String Bridge Ever Made of String?

There are two ways to get across the river in downtown Exeter. The Great Bridge crosses the river at the upper falls and the String Bridge crosses at the lower. Sometimes when people cross the Great Bridge, they don't even realize they've crossed a bridge at all, and certainly don't notice the falls. Great Bridge is our primary bridge in Exeter; perhaps this is why it has such an impressive name. Our waterfalls may not be as spectacular as Niagara Falls, but they're important to us and are the reason the town exists at all. We have every right to call our bridge "Great."

The String Bridge sits over the lower falls at the point where the Exeter River meets the Squamscott River. The first mill ever built in Exeter was built on the little island that makes up the center of the bridge. String Bridge is actually two bridges and an island. When Thomas Wilson first set up his gristmill in the 1640s on the eastern side of the island, he most likely threw together a bridge so his patrons could carry sacks of grain across without needing a boat. This early bridge, although not specifically described in any of the early records, was most likely a narrow pedestrian arrangement made up of a single "stringer" log. So, no, we likely never had a rope bridge crossing the river in Exeter, however romantic that idea may be.

When Captain John Gilman built his gristmill on the western side of the island, he was given the right by the town to build a more substantial bridge. His bridge system was described by Charles Bell as "nothing more than one or two timbers laid across each of the channels of the river, with hand rails at the side." It remained a pedestrian bridge for over one hundred years. This is the bridge that appears on our earliest map of Exeter in 1802.

Around 1817, it was decided to transform the String Bridge, as it was now called due to its early construction, into a carriage bridge. New stringers were installed, with planking laid across wide enough to allow a single horse

The String Bridge in Exeter is actually two bridges, as seen in this early photograph, circa 1860.

and carriage to pass. The construction was paid for by the townspeople of Exeter who made pledges for the cost. This incarnation of the bridge served the town well, even if it did still cause a bit of traffic disruption when two carriages wanted to pass at the same time. By 1888, however, the bridge was showing its age. The *Exeter News-Letter* reported, "On Thursday afternoon of last week Brown & Warren made an examination of the southern portion of String Bridge, finding the planking and cross timbers so unsound as to make the bridge really unsafe." Repairs were ordered immediately. Within a short time, it was determined that simple repairs were not enough and the bridge system was almost entirely rebuilt.

The bridges were enlarged in 1910 to accommodate two carriages to pass, but the structure we know today was eventually built in 1935. If you walk across the bridge today, you can still see this date carved into the railing. The *Exeter News-Letter* boasted at the time, "All materials, where possible, are to be purchased from Exeter merchants."

The island has had many names over the years, usually based on the names of businesses that were located on it. The current agreed-upon designation is "Kimball's Island," named for Kimball's Plumbing. Over the years, the island was used for mills, warehouses and even a blacksmith shop owned by Swedish immigrant, Olaf Hanson. For a while, the address for this business was Chestnut Hill Avenue, but today the simpler String Bridge is used.

Streets and Their Names—Court Street and Pine Street

The joke around the historical society is that here in Exeter, we never lose houses—we just burn 'em or move 'em. With just a few exceptions, this is mostly true. Sure, we tore down the county courthouse on Front Street and the original St. Michael's Church on Center Street was razed after it was sold to the bank, but usually we can track a missing building to a fire scene or an entirely new location.

A similar phenomenon can occur when researching the streets of Exeter. No, we don't burn streets—unlike houses, streets don't disappear—but they do have birthdates and can change names as often as Elizabeth Taylor Hilton Wilding Todd Fisher Burton Burton Warner Fortensky.

If you studied the 1802 map of Exeter and tried to locate Court Street, it might be somewhat surprising to discover that it ran through the center of town. In fact, it would look suspiciously like Front Street, because eventually it would become Front Street. The original courthouse stood blocking traffic in the middle of the street in the same place that the bandstand blocks traffic today. By the 1830s, it was decided that the building, although well built and very useful, was underfoot like a toddler and so it was carefully and slowly moved to "the new road to Kensington," which soon thereafter became known as Court Street. The old Court Street was renamed Front Street and the new road became the Court Street that we know today. Oddly, the courthouse wouldn't remain on Court Street for very long.

A few years after settling onto its new foundation, the courthouse was hired out for a grand exhibition of the *Conflagration of Moscow*, presented in diorama and fantoccini—a kind of automated puppet show. The *Exeter News-Letter* reported on March 9, 1841, that it was "a spectacle most magnificent, impressive, and sublime." Ten days later, both the courthouse and the exhibition burned to the ground in a tremendous fire. "When first

The old courthouse (also known as the town house) on Court Street. It was built in 1841 after a fire destroyed the previous courthouse. Today it is home to the town's senior center.

discovered, the flames were bursting out of the windows, and there was no possibility of saving the building. The *Conflagration of Moscow* had, for several evenings, been exhibited there, and the *finale* of the exhibition was the Conflagration of the Court House." A new building was hastily erected for the court and town meetings, but within ten years it was apparent that it was so flimsy that the second story was in danger of collapse whenever town meetings were held. In a move that is fiscally surprising to us, the town voted to build the expensive and elegant brick town hall that still stands in the center of town, and the old building was used as a school, a firehouse and, today, the senior center. But in spite of the courthouse moving back to Front Street, Court Street has remained Court Street ever since.

Pine Street was originally on the outskirts of town. It was so rural that when Judge Henry Flagg French decided to build a house there in 1850, it was seen as a slightly crazy move. Judge French presided over the court of common pleas, but he also had a fascination with all things agrarian. It was

The French House on its original site on Pine Street. Built in 1850 by Judge Henry Flagg French, father of sculptor Daniel Chester French, it stood in a once-remote part of town.

through his efforts that the center of town was planted with the towering elm trees that were long identified with Exeter. His farm on Pine Street utilized all his studies in agricultural drainage. Before the street was actually given an official name, the town considered calling it "French Street" in his honor. Perhaps he was the one who encouraged the name Pine Street instead. French's reputation in town was later overshadowed—much to his delight—by that of his son, Daniel Chester French. The younger French would become one of the most prominent sculptors of the late nineteenth and early twentieth centuries, producing such works as the Lincoln Memorial in Washington, D.C., and the *Concord Minuteman*.

Pine Street today, with its elegant houses, seems an unlikely location for a working farm, but its woodsy name well illustrates how street names more commonly reflect the past than the present.

Leather Tanning
in Exeter

Most of the streets in Exeter have names that make some sense. Water Street is near the river, Lincoln Street is named for Abraham Lincoln and Court Street at one time had a courthouse. Tan Lane doesn't exactly hand out any clues, although perhaps it would if it had been correctly named Tannery Lane.

Originally, this short little road was called Academy Lane, bordering on Phillips Exeter Academy when the school first held classes in 1783. By 1845, the street was peppered with five leather tanneries and most people in town had begun to call it Tan Lane.

The process of tanning leather, taking a raw animal skin and processing it into useable material, is long, difficult and smelly. The skins were first soaked in a strong lime solution to allow any remaining organic material to rot away. Alternately dried and soaked, the skins were later immersed in a vat of tannic acid—derived from ground tree bark—and scraped to remove all remaining hair and fat. The entire process took months to complete. The fat was sold to the equally pungent soap manufacturers and hair was used for plastering walls. As repulsive as this process may have seemed, it was a vast improvement on the earlier methods of tanning, which required the skins to be soaked alternately in urine and dung. It was still, however, considered an unsavory industry and was usually relegated to the outskirts of town. How was it then, that Exeter's tanneries were established within a quarter mile of the downtown area?

The constant soaking, rinsing, stretching and drying required the tanner to have a reliable source of flowing water. Deep pits were dug into the ground to hold the various solutions and skins. Academy Lane just happened to have two underground springs that provided an ample amount of water. Both emptied into the Squamscott River, a body of water used by most townies at the time as a wastewater drain.

Tan Lane in 1917, then called Academy Lane, during the time when Phillips Exeter Academy was buying the old, decaying remains of Exeter's once-thriving tanning industry. None of the decrepit wooden buildings exist today.

The industry flourished for about fifty years on Academy Lane. Tanners passed the business on to their sons, and the few families that participated in the trade intermarried. Perhaps it took a certain type of person to deal with all that decaying matter. According to Charles Bell, it was Edmund Pearson and his son, Nathaniel, who began building tanneries in Exeter. Jeremiah Dow, Jeremiah Robinson and Retire Parker followed them into the business. John Folsom Moses married Mary Pearson and opened a morocco factory, producing tanned goat and sheepskin. Over the course of his eighty-eight-year lifespan, Moses married twice and produced twenty-five children—more offspring than *Law and Order*.

By 1888, when Bell wrote his *History of the Town of Exeter, New Hampshire*, the tanning industry had ceased to exist in Exeter. Gradually, Phillips Exeter Academy began building on Academy Lane and by the twentieth century owned most of the property. Oddly, although it was never officially called Tan Lane when the tanneries were there, the street's name was changed once the academy moved in. Thus, it was Academy Lane when populated by tanneries, and Tan Lane when all the buildings were academy owned. If this seems wrong somehow, remember that Summer Street and Winter Street are wrong most of the time as well.

THE EXPLODING CANNONS
OF GILMAN PARK

There are a number of scenic spots along the Exeter River, and Gilman Park is probably one of the nicest. Set off of Bell Avenue, the park is a wonderful spot for sports, picnics and light boating.

In 1890, the Exeter Agricultural, Industrial and Town Improvement Association set about to beautify the town. There had been a history of beautification in the town, or "village" as is was often called, going back to the 1840s, when Henry Flagg French had begun planting trees in the downtown area. When it appeared that the river was facing even more deforestation for firewood, the Improvement Association took action and contacted one of the riverfront property owners, Daniel Gilman, with a request that he modify his plans.

Gilman was a wealthy entrepreneur who ran the Rubber Step Manufacturing Company and dabbled in real estate. Descended from the first Gilman family in Exeter, his father had built up an export trade business with China and left his widow, Mary Gray Gilman, and children with a sizeable inheritance. With nothing to loose but a bit of firewood, Gilman agreed to gift ten acres of land at the confluence of the Exeter and Little Rivers for a woodland park—provided the town built a small footbridge to link the park with the village. At the March 1891 town meeting, it was voted to accept Gilman's generous gift and name the spot "Gilman Park."

The park officially opened in July 1892 amid great fanfare. The Exeter Brass Band was on hand to entertain and the spot soon became a favorite among picnickers. By June of 1893, the *Exeter News-Letter* was able to report that "last Sunday over a thousand were counted as they passed down Gilman Street not to mention those who went by boat."

The "rustic footbridge" that Gilman had envisioned has been built, damaged and repaired numerous times over the years, but the real problem

An unidentified man poses with one of the Gilman Park cannons shortly after their arrival in Exeter in 1897.

for the park trustees has always been rubbish and vandals. Early in the park's history, callous visitors would dump trash in the park, spoiling the natural setting. This was during a time period when waste was habitually dumped in unused spaces. Repeated appeals to local civic groups for cleanup days in the park occurred regularly.

Daniel Gilman and family.

In 1897, the United States government offered surplus naval cannons to municipalities for decorative purposes. Exeter applied for two large guns and was rewarded with three, plus sixty-nine cannonballs. Within twenty years the cannonballs had disappeared—mostly tossed into the river by vandals eager to show off their prowess. In 1929, while the town was doing dam repairs, Charles Russell, one of the Gilman Park trustees, managed to recover eighteen of the balls from the river.

The cannons themselves have been attacked by vandals. Although a few concerned citizens felt they should have been used during the Spanish-American War, the cannons have never been recalled for active duty by the government. In 1953, the *Exeter News-Letter* reported that "a loud explosion heard in town about 9 A.M. last Friday was caused by pranksters firing a heavy charge from one of the cannons in Gilman Park. The cannon was forced off its foundation by the force of the explosion."

The cannon survived that particular attack, but in October of 1969, vandals again struck and blew one of the cannons apart completely. The police reported that pieces of the gun were found more than a quarter of a mile away. After that incident, the cannons were disabled and can no longer be fired. The eighteen cannonballs recovered in 1929 are long gone.

The park is still beautiful and you can still see the cannons, although they are best viewed from the river. I rounded the bend in my kayak last year with my younger daughter and we were met with the sight of both cannons leveled right at us. "Ahhhhhhhhhh!" she yelled, "I thought we were gonna see ducks!" Who wants to look at ducks when you can open a conversation about Exeter's exploding cannons?

DICK THE FIRE HORSE

W hy do humans keep pets? I often wonder this when my husband's three completely useless house cats are draped around the living room. He tells me they provide companionship, unconditional love and, best of all, they don't talk back like the kids. Although he may have a point there, particularly the bit about not talking, they still seem overindulged to me. If only we had the sensibilities of our ancestors, who couldn't afford to get attached to their animals. Animals had a purpose back then—either as a worker or a food source. Take Exeter's fire horses as an example.

After a series of devastating downtown fires in the early 1870s, Exeter townsfolk finally put a crowbar into the budget and paid $4,400 for a state-of-the-art steam fire engine. The town engines up until this time were hand-dragged, hand-pumped tubs that were hauled to the scene of the fire by the firemen. The new steamer was purchased in 1873 and could throw seven hundred gallons of water per minute. This allowed firefighters to actually put out a fire instead of simply protecting the surrounding buildings. But the darn thing was heavy and would require horses to pull it.

For seventeen years, the town hired horses from a nearby livery stable. When the fire alarm sounded, someone had to run across the street to get the often-reluctant horses. The steamer itself had to be kindled and primed. By the time all this was done, your house could be in cinders. Larger communities were already acquiring teams of horses for the sole purpose of firefighting. In 1890, Exeter Chief Engineer Charles Warren formally recommended the purchase of a team of town horses. The townsmen agreed and before another month went by a fine matched set of gray Percherons were purchased in Pittsfield.

Firefighters initially distained having to share quarters with mere horses, but fire horses soon proved to be part of the brotherhood. When the alarm sounded, the chains across the horses' stalls would automatically drop, the horses would step into their places and the harness system would drop onto their backs from above. A few quick buckles and the engine would be racing to the fire scene. The horses were often ready before their human counterparts. They had to be brawny enough to pull the big engines and unflappable at a fire scene, where they were often required to stand for hours in the heat of a billowing fire with sparks showering from above—the steamer itself often producing more black smoke than the actual fire.

Exeter's horses were named Dick and Prince, but Dick soon proved to be the town favorite and was generally referred to as "Pet." His intelligence was unsurpassed by any other town horse. John Templeton, the editor of the *Exeter News-Letter* and volunteer firefighter, wrote of Dick in 1896 that the horse was capable of untying his halter to wander around the firehouse, opening doors as he went. If he were really bored, he would open the taps to get a drink and turn on the gaslights. Unfortunately, he never remembered to turn the faucet off again and eventually the annoyed firemen had to box

The members of Exeter's Eagle Steamer Company proudly pose in front of their engine house on Water Street in the 1890s. Dick and Prince, the fire horses, moved just as the photograph was taken (Dick is in the foreground). H.L. Philbrook, the driver, is seated on the steamer. Philbrook was overcome with grief when Dick died after a short illness in 1900.

Dick and Prince were often required to perform highway department work. Here they unenthusiastically pull the water works sprinkler truck.

it in. Templeton went on to say, "Calls for duty at fires being infrequent, he and his mate are regularly worked upon the streets, where Pet is an inveterate beggar of apples, bananas and other tidbits, never losing an opportunity to make for a person in possession of a coveted dainty." He was as gentle as a lamb with his fellow firefighters, who sometimes used him as a chair in the station, yet "no fireman is quicker or more eager to respond to an alarm." It seems fire horses were adrenalin-junkies just like their fellow firefighters.

When Pet died in 1900 at the age of eighteen, the fire department was brokenhearted. His obituary, written by his old friend John Templeton, ran thirty-nine words longer than that of Fire Chief George Carter. "Dick, or Pet as he was commonly addressed, died last Saturday morning, to the intense grief of his driver, Mr. H.L. Philbrook, and hardly less to all members of the steamer company and to many friends in and out of the fire department," it began. His illness had lasted a mere three days and Philbrook was at his side almost the entire time. "A more faithful, capable, docile and intelligent horse than Dick could not easily be found. He did more than his share of the team's work, and instantly responded to every alarm. Prince much feels the separation from his mate of many years." Dick was buried at a local farm.

Prince never worked as a fire horse again. Horses don't take well to new partners and fire horses are nearly impossible to retrain. Many an iceman thought he was getting a great bargain with a retired fire horse only to discover that at the sound of any bell or whistle his wagon would take off at lightning speed, often leaving the driver behind. Prince was sold for twenty-five dollars to the man who provided the new team. He promised the town he would give Prince "kind treatment and a home for life." Good thing people were more sensible and detached about animals back in the good old days.

EXETER NURSES
TRAINING SCHOOL

One hundred years ago, Exeter Cottage Hospital opened the Exeter Nurses Training School, graduating the first class of five nurses three years later in 1909. The nurses were given "a thorough and systematic course of training in medical, surgical, and obstetrical nursing." The hospital itself had just moved into new quarters on Prospect Hill, having outgrown the previous building on Pine Street just eleven years after opening, and it was time to enlarge the nursing staff.

In the early twentieth century, almost all such training was done at hospital-based schools such as Exeter. It not only provided excellent hands-on training for the students but also staffed the hospital. Nursing students paid for their uniforms, stockings and shoes and the hospital provided housing, board and a small stipend. The students had to pay for any equipment breakage out of this stipend. Pauline Kenick, a student at Exeter in the 1930s, said there was usually very little left over. Still, the prospect of compensated training drew many women into nursing.

The young women at Exeter attended lectures in anatomy and physiology; obstetrics for nurses; dietetics; *materia medica* (today called pharmacology); fever nursing; and in the earlier years of the school, reading aloud and massage. All these studies had to be wedged between duty shifts of twelve hours apiece. Although the hospital benefited by having the students available, there was a paid staff on duty as well, and not all the nurses trained at the school stayed on. Many went into private duty nursing and worked at patient's homes—particularly in the days when contagious patients weren't allowed in the hospital for fear of spreading diseases. An entire family might be quarantined at home during an outbreak of measles and private duty nurses were an important part of the public healthcare system.

Graduating nurses from the Exeter Nurses Training School at Exeter Cottage Hospital, 1933.

Eventually, the school sent the students to other institutions for specialized training. Pauline Kenick recalled going on affiliation for three months each in Manchester at the Balch for Pediatrics; Concord at the State Hospital for psychiatric nursing; and Boston City Hospital for contagion. Boston was her least favorite rotation because the hospital neglected to provide meals for night shift nurses.

Most of the students who attended the school were recruited from out of town to protect patient confidentiality. It was believed that town girls would be too familiar with the local population. Exeter trained nurses from as far away as Michigan and even Nova Scotia. They lived at the Tuck Nurses Home on the campus of Exeter Hospital with strict rules regarding behavior and dress. The discipline paid off, as almost all of the students were hired immediately after graduation. They served as staff in hospitals across the country and many put in time during the two world wars. During the 1918 influenza epidemic, four nurses and their supervisor became ill, and a promising student from Canada, Annie Snedden, died from her on-duty exposure.

A student nurse in a rare moment of clowning with an obliging patient in the 1920s at the Exeter Cottage Hospital.

Many of the nurses trained at Exeter formed lifelong friendships and the Alumnae Association became a treasured tie to the past. Although it is spelled incorrectly on the signpost, "Alumni Drive" is named for the graduates of the Exeter Nurses Training School. The school graduated its last class in 1935, but the contributions of these women will not be forgotten. Exeter Hospital unveiled a history wall dedicated to the school and its students in September of 2006.

THIS OLD OUTHOUSE

It can be so easy to overlook the changes in our landscape. It's probable that most people today, viewing the picture on this page, would see the falls at String Bridge with some cute little woodsheds in the foreground. Of course, those are not woodsheds. They are a rarely photographed, but always present, necessity of life—the lowly outhouse.

Outhouses stood behind nearly every business and house in town. Quietly tucked out of view—far enough away to prevent detection on hot days when the windows were open, yet close enough to encourage use during those retentive frigid days of winter—the outhouse was the only option before the arrival of sewers and indoor plumbing. Modern indoor bathrooms were not commonplace until the early 1900s.

An outhouse didn't have to be pretty, but it did have to be sturdy. If one's lot was large enough, the outhouse was simply picked up and moved to another spot if the contents threatened to meet the users. In tighter spaces, the pit had to be emptied by a specialized team of workers who arrived at night and gave the lyrical name of "night soil" to the material they carted away.

Although one might think that the outhouse was no place to linger, an awful lot of activity went on in there. The standard two-seater (one large, one small, to prevent the terrified child from "falling in") was the scene of many family dramas. Farm kids avoided work by hanging around the outhouse. Teenagers would sneak a forbidden cigarette. Parents could drop in for a quick nip in those days of legal temperance. The outhouse was also the place to get rid of unwanted evidence. It's no surprise that the axe used to murder Lizzie Borden's parents was found in the privy pit. Less notorious crimes were also hidden in the pit—the broken remains of grandma's favorite teacup, the empty bottle of Lydia Pinkham's Vegetable Compound and the

A small crowd of people gathers along the falls at the String Bridge in Exeter to watch ice floes head downstream. Unregarded, but caught by the photographer, are two structures in the foreground undeniably necessary for everyday life.

shattered head of your older sister's favorite china doll. As such, the privy is a goldmine for historic archaeologists, who happily trowel away to discover our secret past.

But before we get nostalgic about those simpler times, let's not avoid the health risks involved in our sturdy little structure. Night visits to the outhouse were rare; most people utilized an indoor chamber pot. Each morning, the thunder pot had to be emptied and, unfortunately, this was done after washing up. Breakfast would then be served with a hefty dose of potentially lethal typhoid bacteria. As late as the 1880s, Exeter still listed an average of three typhoid fever deaths per year. The number of recovered cases is unknown, but even one bout with this disease was debilitating. Typhoid is passed only through people and requires direct contact with substances we only discuss with toddlers and medical personnel. The outhouse and its little brother, the chamber pot, were the perfect vectors to aid in transmission of this disease.

The proximity of the pictured outhouses to the river has not missed anyone's notice. It's no wonder the Squamscott River was rarely used for recreational swimming. Fouling one's drinking water was a way of life back in the good old days, as the farmer's outhouse was usually located conveniently near the well. As quaint as it was, it's probably a good thing that the outhouse has vanished from our landscape.

Scottish Prisoners

in Exeter

Hello, I'm looking for the burial site of Alexander Gordon." This frequent phone query sometimes makes me want to record the following message on our answering machine: "You have reached the Exeter Historical Society, we are open for genealogical research but we do not know where Alexander Gordon is buried."

Alexander Gordon was the first Gordon to come to America, and I realize that it is important for his genealogically curious descendants to want to find his final resting place. It's just that we really don't know exactly where he is buried. The best we can do is direct them to the Perkins Hill Cemetery, formerly the Gordon Hill Cemetery, and reassure them that Alexander Gordon's son, Thomas, left his entire estate, including "half an acre of land to be reserved for a Burying place," to his own sons. As he had inherited the land from his father, it is more than likely that somewhere on the hill is the final resting place of Alexander Gordon. If it is, then Perkins Hill is the setting for the final chapter of a very exciting biography.

From Scotland, there was very little immigration to New England in the early 1600s. The Scots were usually Presbyterians who tended to clash with New England Puritans. They also didn't speak English; they spoke a form of Highland Gaelic, which may surprise many people today. During the volatile period of the English civil war, Oliver Cromwell's forces attacked Scotland not once but twice, both resulting in crushing Scottish defeats. At both the Battles of Dunbar, in 1650, and Worcester, in 1651, thousands of very young Scotsmen were marched to England as prisoners of war. Most of them were in their teens and early twenties and it would have been dangerous to allow them to return to Scotland after the war ended. Angry young men tend to hold a grudge. The decision was made to sell the able-bodied into servitude in the colonies.

Fifteen-year-old Alexander Gordon was caught up in the conflict. Marched miserably to London to await transportation, he survived the cold and near starvation long enough to win a miserable three-to-four-month cruise on a fetid, overcrowded slave ship bound for the wilderness of America. Upon arrival in Massachusetts, he was sold for between fifteen and thirty pounds for six years of unpaid service. Americans were quite used to the systems of slavery and indentured servitude, but the Scotsmen were not. They tried, unsuccessfully, to use the colonial legal system to shorten their terms of service. Gordon himself filed suit in 1654 against John Cloyce, claiming he had been defrauded. Most of these cases were dismissed. After his attempt to manipulate the legal system, Gordon disappears from the record, only to reappear in 1664 in Exeter, New Hampshire. There we find him working at the sawmill of Nicholas Lissen on the Exeter River.

Lissen, an Englishman by birth, seems to have preferred the company of Scottish prisoners of war. He hired, or perhaps bought indentures of, at least three of them—Gordon, John McBean and Henry Magoon. Conveniently, Lissen had three daughters, and one after another married the Scotsmen. Hannah married John Bean (he dropped the "Mc") in 1654, Elizabeth and Henry Magoon were wed in 1657 and Mary married Alexander Gordon in 1663. One way to escape servitude, apparently, was to marry the owner's daughter. All three men became landowners and partners in the sawmill. Another former prisoner in Exeter was John Sinkler, who worked in a sawmill on the other side of town.

The Scotsmen who came to Exeter all stayed and became equal citizens. According to Diane Rapaport, a writer on the subject, "There is little evidence that any of the men went back to Scotland" after they had served their time. "What happened to the Scotsmen at that point varied greatly, depending upon who had owned them and where, whether they could read or write, and how well they could speak English." The Lissen sisters must have been good teachers, because not only are there still a lot of Beans and Magoons living in New England, the Gordon family returns to Exeter with some regularity to visit the spot where Alexander might be buried.

THE MYSTERIOUS
DOCTOR WINDSHIP

When Phineas Merrill created his map of Exeter in 1802, he was careful to label all the buildings and residents in town. Although the Exeter Historical Society is familiar with most of the people he named, one man stumped our research for many years—the mysterious Doctor Windship of Water Street.

According to Merrill, he lived in a house that once stood across from the current entrance to Swasey Parkway, but he isn't listed on the U.S. census of 1800 or 1810. Charles Bell's *History of Exeter* doesn't mention him as one of the early physicians in the town, and deed research indicated that Doctor Windship never owned the house. It belonged to Widow Stacy. Well, so what? Why should anyone care about a guy who rented a house in town over two hundred years ago? We'd never had a genealogist come looking for him. We didn't even know the guy's first name.

In the spring of 2004, the historical society hired Laura Martin Gowing as our new program manager and she brought with her an almost unnatural interest in Doctor Windship. She quickly discovered, as we had previously, that there seemed to be no clues regarding the man. He was just a name on a map. One day, while poking through an old newspaper, I happened on a column entitled, "Rockingham's Rambles," which was excerpting the diary of Solon Stevens. Most of it contained dull entries like, "Rode with Betsey round the Plains," but there was also this entry: "March 28, 1804: Attended the funeral of my old landlady Mrs. Windship who died suddenly in a fit Monday night." Hmm…Windship…Windship…where had I heard that name before? I casually mentioned the entry to Laura and it wasn't long before we'd found Mrs. Elizabeth Windship lying peacefully in the old Exeter Cemetery on Winter Street. Her grave marker listed her as the daughter of Ephraim May, Esq., of Boston. A quick search of Massachusetts records provided her marriage to Doctor Amos Windship in Roxbury in 1784.

Amos Windship turned out to be quite a guy. Variously described as "thief, fraudster and attempted bigamist," he also served as a surgeon with the American forces during the Revolution. After the Battle of Breed's Hill (or Bunker Hill, if you're lost in Boston), George Washington wrote to John Hancock: "Doctr Winship who lodg'd in the same House with an Officer of the Marines assures me thy had exactly 1043 killed & wounded, of whom 300 fell on the Field or died within a few Hours. Many of the wounded are since dead." Respected by the Americans, he was also admired by the British when, in 1791, he arranged to have the remains of one Major John Pitcairn returned to England for internment in the family plot. Pitcairn had fallen during the Battle of Breed's Hill and died shortly thereafter. His grateful family believed that Windship had done them a gracious favor.

But there are a number of gaping holes in the story of this respectable war veteran. In Boston's Old North Church lies the crypt of Major John Pitcairn—it seems that Amos Windship had failed to send the correct body and Bostonians still believe that Pitcairn resides in the basement. There is a marker on the crypt reading, in part: "Major John Pitcairn, fatally wounded while rallying the Royal Marines at the Battle of Bunker Hill, He died June 17, 1775 and his body was interred beneath this church."

Windship's family life is also genealogical nightmare. Along with Elizabeth May, he seems to have had overlapping wives at various times—two of whom appear to have been sisters. This might explain why Elizabeth's grave marker reads: "erected by her children in 1809." With the exception of an altercation with Moses Thurston over the illegal impounding of a pig, Windship seems to have behaved himself in Exeter. We're able to guess that he arrived in the town sometime around 1802 and left before the 1810 census. But what, Laura wondered, would have brought this colorful character to Exeter? In combing through the available records, we were able to locate two students attending Phillips Exeter Academy during Windship's short stay in town: John Cravath May Windship, aged thirteen, and Letsom Windship, aged twelve. John would go on to Harvard, graduating in 1809. He moved to Louisiana, where he worked as a lawyer until his early death in 1814. Perhaps, like so many other families, the Windships had moved to town to take advantage of the education offered by Phillips Exeter Academy. Or perhaps Windship was avoiding the anger of two other wives. We may never know.

After Elizabeth's death, he married again and moved to Roxbury, where he died in 1813—a remarkable and still somewhat mysterious man who brought his colorful story to Exeter simply by living on Water Street when a mapmaker came through.

LEWIS CASS

S ometimes finding the story of a town's favorite son can be as awkward as coming across pictures of oneself from the disco era. Surely those rhinestone-encrusted bell-bottomed jeans looked ridiculous even back then? Sadly, no one else in the picture is flinching—the clothes, the dancing and the music were all socially acceptable and were even considered, dare we say it, "normal." Who are we to judge?

The more I learn about Exeter's Lewis Cass, the more I get that vague, creepy feeling that here was a man of great convictions. He was a thoroughly honorable man, well grounded in his Puritan roots, a teetotaler and fully dedicated to two basic life tenants: Great Britain was evil and had evil intent in all discourse; and the greatest document ever written was the United States Constitution. What a shame that he was also a slaveholder, voted for the Fugitive Slave Act and participated in the forced migration of the native population—the "Trail of Tears." It can make you wonder why we couldn't get a better hero for our town.

Cass was born on Cross Street on October 9, 1782, during that difficult time after independence had been won but before the Constitution had been written. Politically, it was a bit like having a substitute teacher for seven years. Nothing seemed to run smoothly and Lewis Cass later remembered that one of his earliest memories was of looking out the window of his house at the bonfires lit downtown to celebrate New Hampshire's casting the deciding vote to ratify the new Constitution. That's a pretty symbolic early memory, considering mine are mostly reruns of *Gilligan's Island*. Lewis was the eldest son of a Revolutionary War soldier named Jonathan Cass and Mary Gilman. Jonathan craved excitement and young Lewis must have had a bit of his father's enthusiasm because at the early age of nine, his father enrolled him in the new Phillips Exeter Academy to tame him. Dr. Abbott was able to

Lewis Cass.

teach the young man Greek, Latin, French, geography, geometry, rhetoric and moral philosophy, but failed to manage his atrocious penmanship.

While Lewis Cass attended the academy, his family moved west. He followed them soon after graduation through several states, eventually arriving in Ohio, where he studied for and passed the Ohio Bar—the first person to do so in this new territory. Eventually landing in Michigan, Cass was one of the most educated people there. He was responsible for treaties with the native populations of the territory—always treating the people fairly in spite of his natural dislike for such an "uncivilized race." He married Elizabeth Spencer in 1806, and little is known of their personal life except

Birthplace of Lewis Cass on Cass Street in Exeter.

that it seems to have been harmonious. He served during the War of 1812, a war he generally disapproved of, and attained the rank of brigadier general. It was during this time that Cass developed his strong dislike for the British. He was appointed governor of the Michigan Territory in 1813, became secretary of war under President Jackson and accepted a post as ambassador to France in 1836. Fluent in French, he took this job a bit too seriously, writing all his dispatches in French until he was told to knock it off by the American Foreign Office. Eventually, he meddled too often in foreign policy and resigned in a huff.

He returned to the United States in 1842, considered a hero by many. It was around this time that his hometown renamed Cross Street "Cass Street" in his honor. He ran for president a few times, always supporting the constitutional right of the Southern states to own slaves. In his view, the Union could only be preserved by conceding this right to the slave states; new states, he felt, had a right to choose whether they wished to be slave or free. James Buchanan appointed him secretary of state during his difficult presidency. Cass was a strong supporter of the Dred Scott decision, which denied blacks the right to citizenship, and he refused to issue any passports to free black citizens during his time in office. He outlived his old friend and rival, Daniel Webster, by fourteen years, living long enough to see his precious Union preserved not by concessions but by blood during the Civil War.

Cass is still highly regarded in Michigan and on Cass Street in Exeter, where his birthday is still celebrated to this day.

IN SEARCH
OF THE *Sunbeam*

The story of Captain John Chadwick and the sinking of the ship *Sunbeam* has been told in Exeter for over a century. Chadwick was an Exeter boy who took to sea at the age of eighteen. By the 1870s, he was a well-established sea captain working for the shipping firm of Hemmenway & Browne of Boston. In early 1870, he set sail for South America on the *Sunbeam*, accompanied by his fourteen-year-old son, Alfred, and sixteen other crew members. The voyage was uneventful until noontime on March 31, when Chadwick ordered his second mate to clean and varnish the deck. He dutifully swept the deck and went into the hold to collect the varnish, making the tremendous mistake of taking "an open flame," perhaps a candle or lantern, with him. This was about as smart as smoking a cigarette while pumping gas—the hold of the *Sunbeam* on that day was packed not only with barrels of varnish but also six hundred tons of saltpeter recently loaded aboard in Inquique, Peru. Unsurprisingly, a huge explosion soon shook the ship and Captain Chadwick later commented that it was impossible to fight the flames or even launch the lifeboats as "the flames were rushing in fearful volumes from all parts of the ship and many explosions were going on below."

Captain Chadwick, his son and a seaman remained onboard the burning vessel until all hope was gone. When he realized the ship was lost, he commanded the seaman to launch a piece of the sail yard, a spar, into the water. Seizing young Alfred, he jumped into the water to join the other crew members now clinging to wreckage. By chance, a single boat had dropped flaming into the water in an upright position. One of the sailors managed to put out the flames and climb aboard to rescue anyone he could find. Chadwick and Alfred were found still clutching the spar with the unnamed seaman. Several hours later, the whaling bark, *Charles W. Morgan*, having seen the smoke while looking for more whales to harpoon, picked up the survivors

Captain John Chadwick was a well-established sea captain from Exeter who worked for the shipping firm of Hemmenway & Browne of Boston.

The Chadwick House on Front Street in Exeter. This is now the site of the Exeter Inn, behind which stands a flagpole with a replica of the Chadwick Spar.

and ferried them to the nearest port. Somehow in all the chaos, Captain Chadwick had the presence of mind to rescue the spar that had saved young Alfred and himself. He shipped it back to Exeter and had it erected at the top of a flagpole in front of his house on Pine Street where it remained as a local landmark.

Also on board the *Sunbeam* for that fateful voyage was a young man named Marshall Johnson, who would go on to become a well-known maritime painter. He created a glorious painting of the sinking of the *Sunbeam* for the offices of Hemmenway & Browne, who accepted it graciously in spite of its depiction of one of the worst disasters the firm had ever weathered. The painting eventually made its way to the Chadwick Room of the Exeter Inn on Front Street. The Exeter Inn had been built by Phillips Exeter Academy in the 1930s on the site of the old Chadwick Home. The flagpole, with the decaying remains of the lifesaving spar, remained in the backyard, somewhat forgotten.

Neither Chadwick nor his son ever put to sea again. Captain Chadwick took a desk job with the firm and commuted to Boston daily by rail. Alfred became a businessman and lived a long and prosperous life.

Knowing this story so well, I naturally had to locate all the elements, as any good tourist of history might. Before visiting the spar, I decided to check out the painting of the *Sunbeam* at the Inn of Exeter. There are black and white photos of it at the Exeter Historical Society and I was itching to see it in color.

"I don't think that one's here anymore," Margaret at the desk informed me. "When the academy sold the inn, most of the paintings were taken out." We walked through the building admiring lots of art, but none of it was of a doomed, burning ship with survivors in the water clinging to a spar. "Try the academy library," she told me.

There are no paintings of the *Sunbeam* at the academy library, either, it turns out, as documents in the archives indicate that the painting had been sold in 1979—coincidentally the same year the flagpole with the rotting remains of the Chadwick spar had collapsed in the backyard of the Exeter Inn. I was devastated to find that the spar was gone. It seems that 1979 was the date of death for the Chadwick Spar and the story of the *Sunbeam* in Exeter.

Heroically for our town's history, in 1984 the Chadwick family, Phillips Exeter Academy and the Exeter Historical Society reerected the flagpole on Pine Street with a replica of the original spar. It might not be the actual artifact, but it's still enough to warrant standing at the base of the pole retelling the story to eager young ears. And that's better than any old pirate story.

GENERAL MARSTON'S
MISSING STATUE

O ne of the most enduring mysteries in Exeter is the missing Civil War
statue from the grave of General Gilman Marston. The statue has
been gone for at least eighty years, perhaps more, and its disappearance is
still unsolved. Most of our cold cases at least have a theory, conspiracy or
not, of how and why it occurred, but this one is stone-cold dead.

Gilman Marston came to Exeter in 1841 when he was a twenty-nine-
year-old lawyer. Born in Orford, he was raised as a farmer's son. He
graduated from Dartmouth and a branch of Harvard Law School. He set
up practice in Exeter, sleeping in his office to save money. His early cases
were small, but gradually he built up the practice while juggling a political
career. Originally a Whig, Marston believed, like most legal men in the early
nineteenth century, that slavery was deplorable but perfectly legal. When
the Republican Party evolved in the 1850s, Marston, a firm supporter of the
Union, joined without hesitation. He served in state government and in 1859
went to Washington, D.C., to serve in the House of Representatives. As the
feeble government of James Buchanan froze in the headlights of secession,
Marston—whom Perley Gardner described as "petulant, explosive, high-
strung, impatient, sharp-tongued, erratic and emotional"—headed back to
Exeter to organize the Second New Hampshire regiment in spite of the fact
that he had no military training and was forty-nine years old at the time. He
remained a member of Congress during his military service and rose to the
rank of brigadier general.

With his raw troops, Marston saw his first action at the Battle of Bull
Run. He was wounded in the right arm during the battle and endured
a harrowing ambulance ride before receiving any medical attention.
Marston refused amputation and kept his arm, but his fingers never worked
properly again. His already poor handwriting suffered badly, which is why

This Civil War statue from the grave of General Gilman Marston has been missing for about eighty years and remains one of Exeter's unsolved mysteries.

his war diaries, now housed at the Exeter Historical Society, are useless as documentary sources.

After the war, Gilman Marston returned to Exeter and resumed his law practice. He stayed in town for the remainder of his life, speaking little of his war experience. He bought a house on Court Street but never married. When he died in 1890 at the age of seventy-nine, the will requested that a simple boulder mark his grave. His grateful regiment complied. Several years later, his friend Stephen Gale decided that a more fitting monument was needed. Gale ordered a standard life-sized Union infantry soldier statue in bronze to stand atop Marston's boulder. It was erected in time for the Memorial Day celebrations in 1896.

The soldier stood six feet tall and was fixed to the boulder with a base three inches thick. The entire thing must have been tremendously heavy. The *Exeter News-Letter* ran one of its earliest photographs of the statue in the June 26, 1896 edition. For a long time, this grainy photo and a heavily retouched postcard were the only proof of the statue's existence. Rummaging through the archives one day, I came across another photo of the statue. These bits

General Gilman Marston. Forty-nine years old when the war broke out, Marston joined up immediately and was quickly made an officer in spite of having no military training.

of evidence are notable because there is no trace of the statue today and no clue as to what happened to it.

How could a heavy six-foot bronze statue just disappear? Two years ago, we decided to reopen the case and find out what had become of it. We determined that the statue must have been gone by 1920, since no living person in Exeter remembers seeing it. No one even remembered hearing about it. No one's grandfather ever sat in a rocking chair, drinking a beer, reminiscing, "I remember when me and Cal dressed up General Marston's soldier like a girl. Good times. Good times." So we combed through every inch of the *Exeter News-Letter*'s "Town Affairs" sections, covering a period of roughly forty years. This was the part of the paper that announced when the rhododendrons bloomed. Nothing got past editor John Templeton—except the strange disappearance of a Civil War statue. There was no notice that it had been stolen, destroyed by lightning, scrapped during World War I or II, removed by angry relatives or melted down to build the Gale Park statue. Judy Dufour checked the cemetery records and they too are remarkably silent. What the heck? How can such a landmark disappear? It's not like the statue was in a deserted part of town. We still end the Memorial Day parade right in front of General Marston's boulder. The only conclusion we've been able to reach is that the statue existed at one time and does not exist anymore. At least not here. Check your neighbor's backyard for us. It's gotta be somewhere.

THE INNOVATIVE MIND OF
BENJAMIN CLARK GILMAN

There's a tall grandfather clock quietly ticking in the main meeting room of the Exeter Historical Society. Recently donated by George Fanning, a descendant of the Pollard and Wadleigh families of Exeter and Newfields, it was built in the late eighteenth century by a remarkable craftsman named Benjamin Clark Gilman.

Gilman was born in Exeter in 1763 in the big house on Cass Street, the twelfth child of John and Jane Gilman. His father was an officer during the French and Indian War, but young Benjamin wasn't much interested in a career in the military. After attending Phillips Exeter Academy, he briefly turned to silversmithing, quickly outshining, as it were, the quality and designs of his older brother's silver work. Perhaps it was sibling rivalry that nudged young Benjamin out of the world of artistic silverwork—we'll never know. But in any case, Benjamin became interested in clocks. His advertisement, placed in 1791, was encouraging: "Those who wish to purchase either large or small eight-day clocks or time-pieces, may depend on having them warranted to be well made and keep regular time. The price will be reasonable, and payments made easy to purchasers, either in cash, country produce or foreign articles." We don't know how the Wadleigh family paid for our clock, but it's still keeping accurate time over two hundred years later.

By the time Gilman began making his clocks, he had also married. Years later, he would still marvel at how strongly he felt about his children: "When Clarissa was about three years old I went from home and was detained two nights. My affections were then so remarkably attached to her that it seemed as though no inducement could ever prevail on me ever to part with her for the space of a fortnite." The family would grow to include eight children. Although Gilman may have been hard put to leave little Clarissa for a few

Benjamin Clark Gilman in a portrait completed during his lifetime by Henry Folsom in 1814.

weeks, his work would take him to neighboring towns for stretches of time because by the early 1800s, he'd again switched vocations. His interest in timepieces had led him to branch into navigational instruments. From there, he took a leap and won a contract to build the lighthouse on New Castle Island at the entrance to Portsmouth Harbor in 1803. Completed in 1804, the lighthouse stood until the Civil War.

Tall case clock, circa 1790, built by Benjamin Clark Gilman. Still in working condition, it can be seen at the Exeter Historical Society.

Like engineers everywhere, Gilman couldn't help tinkering with projects. When the city of Portsmouth needed a way to get fresh drinking water into downtown, Gilman was the one hired to build a wooden aqueduct system. He built the same kind of system in downtown Exeter, drawing water from the west end of town. He used pine logs with a four-inch bore as pipes for his system. Lead pipes brought the water into basement cisterns from which homeowners would either haul or pump to the upper floors. Wooden pipes weren't foolproof—they frequently leaked at the joints and the roots of trees tended to puncture them—but Gilman preferred them to the all-lead system that was in use in some communities. He said that earthworms tended to eat the lead but seemed to dislike pine. He created five aqueduct systems in all: Portsmouth; Exeter; Boston; Salem, Massachusetts; and New London, Connecticut.

Gilman spent his later years in his house on Front Street living with his daughters. He continued to build his tall clocks and served as a town selectman. He died in 1835, but unlike the grandfather's clock in the song, his clocks didn't "stop short, never to go again when the old man died." Every hour when the clock chimes at the historical society, we are reminded of this remarkable craftsman. It is almost as though we hear his voice through the centuries.

Daniel Chester French and the World War I Memorial

S hortly after World War I, the citizens of Exeter met to consider the erection of a memorial dedicated to those who had served overseas. There were a number of ideas bandied about—a statue next to town hall, a new wing on the public library, a community house, just to name a few. All were flavored with the practicality and patriotism of the times.

"What more suitable than a Memorial Community House used to perpetuate this idea, to help care for the young people of the home town of the boys who so bravely did their part?" wrote Kate Hatch to the editor of the *Exeter News-Letter*. A monument, many believed, would honor only the dead and not the living. "A monument is at best but a larger tombstone. If the artist lacks the divine spark, if the monument, which in a drawing looked fair enough, fails when completed to bear the critical test of time, then the town finds itself cursed with an ugly pile of stone in its front yard so long as stone shall endure. These monstrosities we see almost everywhere, dishonoring the dead whom they commemorate and distressing the living," commented Frederick Libby a few weeks after Miss Hatch.

As much as people supported the idea of a grand community house, there was also a sense that some type of monument was needed to draw attention to the great sacrifice made by so many soldiers, sailors and nurses. After numerous meetings failed to reach a consensus, Exeter author and judge Henry A. Shute wrote in favor of both a monument and a meeting place for ex-servicemen instead of the community house. He likened the community house idea as "somewhat analogous to that of the fond wife that buys her husband a vanity bag for a Christmas present, or of the husband that buys his wife a smoking set as an appropriate observance of that occasion."

Daniel Chester French, sculptor, and Alice Gale Hobson, land donor, pose before Exeter's World War I Memorial after the unveiling ceremony on July 4, 1922.

"And our town today has, I believe, the opportunity of obtaining a masterpiece by as great an artist as either of these men (St. Gaudens or Whistler), and a native son, a man that stands at the head of living artists, Daniel Chester French."

French was indeed a native son. Born in 1850 in Exeter, he grew up on Pine Street and attended the Grove Street School. After moving away from town at the age of ten, he went on to become a world-renowned sculptor, completing pieces such as the *Concord Minuteman* (when he was just twenty-four years old) and *George Washington* in Paris, France. In 1920, when Exeter's memorial committee approached him, he had just finished his work on the seated Abraham Lincoln statue for Washington D.C.'s Lincoln Memorial. The Lincoln was at the stonecutter's studio in New York by then and French could only wait to see the finished result.

The town voted to appropriate $20,000 for the statue and an additional $10,000 to renovate the top floor of the town hall for the veterans' use. French agreed to do the work, even though the amount earmarked for the project was far below what it would cost. It would be his gift to the town.

Several sites were considered for the monument. The first choice was near the town hall—after all, that was where the new servicemen's hall would be located. French was unhappy with the site. It was too cramped for his proposed seven-foot statue. He wandered around town in June of 1920, looking for just the right place. Eventually, he suggested either the island on String Bridge or the triangle of land at the meeting of Front and Linden Streets. Front Street, he felt, would bookend the historic part of town between the bandstand and the new monument. Alice Gale Hobson, who owned that particular spit of land, quickly offered to donate it and have an old house removed from the site. French sent for his architect partner, Henry Bacon, who laid out the grounds and built the pedestal.

By spring of 1922, the monument was ready. Originally hoping to unveil it on Memorial Day, the ceremony was put off until July 4 because French and Bacon were attending the opening ceremonies at the Lincoln Memorial. Though French's working title for the statue was *Exeter War Memorial Group*, the town quickly called it *Mother Town Sending her Intrepid Son to War*. Typically French, it exudes elegance. *Mother Town* is a strong, classically clad woman. The soldier (French had him remove his uniform hat in the final version to make him less martial) is a typical town son—erect, yet with the slightest hint of disquietude about his immediate future. It is the town that gives him courage. As Albertus T. Dudley commented at the dedication, "We need no guide to point out to us the beauty of the design or the perfection of its execution. He who stands may read."

HOW TO CHANGE A DUMP
INTO A PARK

If you were to read newspaper accounts of Exeter in the 1930s, you might never know that there was a nationwide economic depression. The stock market crash wasn't considered local news so it didn't make the papers. There were only two bank failures in the entire state of New Hampshire. The 1930 census reported that Exeter's population had finally begun to rise, reversing a decline that had been occurring for decades. Things were looking pretty rosy.

Of course, this wasn't the true picture. Most of New England had been experiencing an economic downturn since the close of World War I. Unemployment was high, workers pulled up stakes in search of better wages and there was little money in circulation. The 1930s didn't really hit with any great force in New England, it was merely an extension of already-existing conditions. What Exeter really needed was a millionaire.

Ambrose Swasey was born in Exeter in 1847, the ninth of ten children. His family lived on the northern edge of town at Fort Rock Farm. As a boy, Swasey attended the Plains School on Park Street and showed an affinity for mechanics. Although his education was short-lived, Swasey landed a job at the Exeter Machine Works when he was eighteen. There he met another bright young man, Worcester R. Warner, and the two became lifelong friends, perhaps because they both bore ridiculous given names. Together they worked and studied and invented improvements on the machines they were building. By 1900, the firm of Warner and Swasey (you'll note they did not call it Ambrose and Worcester) was successfully producing machine tools, instruments of precision and telescopes in their Cleveland headquarters.

Swasey's self-taught engineering brought him fame and considerable fortune. He held six honorary degrees and memberships in numerous engineering and scientific societies, including the National Academy of Sciences and the American Philosophical Society. He was a Fellow of the Royal Astronomical

Historically Speaking

Dedication day for Swasey Parkway in Exeter, November 10, 1930. While the Great Depression loomed in the background, Exeter's citizens were comforted by Ambrose Swasey's generous beautification of the decaying waterfront. Swasey is the fifth man from the left.

Society and Officer of the Legion of Honor (France). But even though he had worldwide acclaim and a fine home in Cleveland, Swasey still frequently returned to Exeter. A devout Baptist, he was a generous supporter of the Exeter Baptist Church. In 1916, he donated to Exeter the elegant Swasey Pavilion, locally known as "the Bandstand," to replace the rickety wooden one that threatened to collapse with every concert. By 1929, he needed a new project. Widowed and with no children to support, he adopted Exeter as his legacy.

One of his biggest irritations when visiting Exeter was the miserable drive from downtown to his home at Fort Rock Farm. The area along the river front had been a thriving shipyard in Revolutionary times and was later an active seaport. By the early twentieth century, the area was the town dump—garbage piled up along the rough shoreline and rats were plentiful. Exeter residents complained that the smell of the river would sometimes waft all the way up to the town hall. But who had money for a cleanup in those times of economic depression?

Swasey made an offer that the town couldn't refuse: he would donate all the money needed to clean up the waterfront and create a parkway open to the public. He would endow the park with funds to provide for its upkeep. Designed by the Olmstead Brothers firm in Boston, the Exeter Shore Parkway, as it was originally named, took three years to complete. The Squamscott River was dredged to deepen the channel, the riverbank was strengthened and retaining walls were constructed. The Furnald House had to be moved to the top of Secretary Hill and several other homes on Water Street were razed to provide access. In November of 1931, the parkway was finally ready. By a unanimous vote, the name was changed to Swasey Parkway in honor of its eighty-four-year-old benefactor.

EXETER'S UNCOMMON DENTIST—CHARLES GERRISH

C harles Bell, in his *History of Exeter*, tells us that the first dentist in town was Dr. Joseph Patch, who set up shop in 1838. At that time, the standard treatment for tooth problems was to pull the tooth. Most adults had few teeth left by the time they reached their fifties. Dr. Patch—even without anesthetics—would have been a much better option than going to the blacksmith, as people would have done before his arrival.

After his arrival, Exeter, like most American towns, has had at least one dentist working in the town at any given time. One of the most colorful dentists was Charles Gerrish, who practiced dentistry for over fifty years. Just before he died in 1918 at the age of seventy-three, Dr. Gerrish wrote to the *Exeter News-Letter*, reassuring his patients that he hoped to be back at his practice soon. His obituary, and the numerous testimonials printed with it, proves that his patients would have been more than willing to accept his treatment.

Gerrish was not born in Exeter, but we won't hold that against him. He was orphaned at the age of six in his hometown of Newburyport and came to Exeter in 1851 to live with his relatives, Mr. and Mrs. Ira Burnham. The Burnhams were the caretakers of Phillip Exeter Academy's Abbot Hall and this was where the young Gerrish grew up. He loved the outdoors and became a superior marksman. After attending Exeter schools, he left to study dentistry.

Like many doctors, dentists and lawyers, Gerrish didn't attend any type of college or university. It was more accepted to receive one's education by studying with an established dentist. We don't know who Gerrish apprenticed with, but when he opened his own practice back in Exeter, he gave as reference Dr. W.H. Noyes of Newburyport.

Dr. Gerrish was a very unusual dentist for his time in that he recommended preventive dentistry. But it took some convincing—most people didn't pay

Doctor Charles Gerrish leads the parade on his bicycle with the town police force behind him on Independence Day 1897.

much attention to their teeth until they were in pain. Gerrish tried to convince them that oral health could influence overall health: "When we consider how essential a thorough mastication of the food is to a healthy condition of the digestive organs and the system in general, we see the importance of preserving our own teeth, or if we are toothless, the securing of artificial teeth, which should by no means depreciate from the worth of natural teeth." He encouraged "the daily use of the tooth brush so indispensable to a healthy condition of the mouth." Americans weren't convinced that brushing their teeth was all that important. The practice didn't catch on with the general public until after World War I, when soldiers returning from war brought with them government-issued toothbrushes.

Gerrish would have spent his days creating dentures and plates for those who didn't follow his good advice. If this became tiresome, he had plenty of hobbies to keep him busy. Gerrish used his boyhood love of shooting to reinvigorate the Exeter Sportsmans Club, captaining the Exeter team all the way to the First International Clay Pigeon Tournament held at Chicago in 1884. Along with four other local men, they won the tournament. He entertained many patients with his tales of trap and game shooting while

An avid sportsman, Doctor Gerrish captained the team from the Exeter Sportsmans Club that won first place in the International Clay Pigeon Tournament held in Chicago in 1884.

he drilled out their cavities and packed their teeth with fillings—all without Novocain, of course.

He also loved the newfangled sport of bicycling, even participating in Exeter's Independence Day parade on one of the new fragile-looking set of wheels. Gerrish was an avid tinkerer, as described by Frederick Charles: "If the dental manufacturers did not have the instruments he desired, his mechanical ingenuity and skillful hands could devise and make them." Imagine, for a moment, arriving at your dentist's office today and having a piece of homemade equipment approach your mouth. People trusted Dr. Gerrish.

He was musical, as was his wife and their only daughter, Charlotte. The family played often for the Congregational Church and Gerrish was a frequent conductor at the town's minstrel shows. Aging didn't slow up his practice, but cancer of the jaw did. After seemingly successful surgery at the Carney Hospital in Boston, he wrote to the town to tell them he was "holding up well under the treatment...As I look back a half century of dental practice in your midst...my aims have been high, they have enabled me to demonstrate to the dental profession the great benefit of preventive dentistry." He developed pneumonia after his surgery, from which he did not recover. However, his enthusiasm for both his town and profession guaranteed that he would not be forgotten by his devoted patients.

DOCTOR ALICE CHESLEY

O live Tardiff's best memory of Dr. Alice Chesley is of a heavyset woman who drove her own car. Women who entered the medical profession in the early twentieth century needed to be tough and independent. Exeter's Dr. Chesley seems to have been no exception to this rule.

When Alice Chesley first moved to Exeter with her parents in 1882 at the age of twenty, the town already had a history of excellent medical care. There had been gifted doctors since the mid-1700s—some of whom are still remembered today, such as Dr. William Perry, for whom the Perry Medical Services Building is named. We could also boast of Dr. David Gorham and Dr. Edward Otis, a noted authority on the treatment of tuberculosis. All were fine doctors, but the unbroken line of trained physicians was most decidedly male.

We have no record of what drove Alice Chesley to seek medical training. After finishing high school in Massachusetts, Chesley studied at the Gorham Normal School in Maine (today part of the University of Maine) and taught public school around New Hampshire for a few years. She found herself working in the Exeter probate office before packing up for the University of Michigan Medical School in 1896. Her education was interrupted briefly two years later when she returned east after her father's death. Once her family affairs were settled, she completed her degree in 1898 and opened practice in 1900.

Although Elizabeth Blackwell had become the first American woman to earn a medical degree some fifty years earlier, it was still unusual to find women in medical school in the 1890s. Blackwell was only accepted to the Geneva Medical School in New York because the trustees put it to a student vote and they believed her application to be a joke. When it turned out that she was a serious student, she was still frequently refused entry to the

Doctor Alice Chesley.

anatomy lab on the grounds that a lady shouldn't be exposed to such things. By the 1890s, Chesley probably didn't encounter such nonsense, but her motivation was most likely questioned.

Returning to Exeter in 1900, Dr. Chesley set up practice in town with Dr. Mary Giles of Malden, Massachusetts. The two briefly moved their office to Malden, but Chesley seems to have been attached to Exeter and returned soon after. For the next forty years, she was a fixture in the healthcare system of Exeter. She worked as the on-call doctor for the Robinson Female Seminary and the University of New Hampshire while maintaining a busy practice in town. For many people, she might not have been the first doctor called—there was still a widespread belief that male doctors were superior practitioners—but she would always arrive when needed. The *Exeter News-Letter* noted after a large snowstorm in 1923 that "Dr. Alice Chesley made a house call to Stratham, it took most of the afternoon; four horses and seven men working in relays were needed to get her there and back." And, of course, as noted earlier, she drove her own car. Nancy Merrill, our town historian who started her career as a school nurse, noted Chesley's devotion to women's health: "Before there were facilities for unwed mothers, she helped many pregnant girls find someplace to stay. One such home was that of Margaret and Sam Cote on Washington Street. They never learned the true identity of their 'house guest,' who enjoyed the benefits of good food, exercise, and a happy family during her stay." We can presume that Dr. Chesley would be the one attending the delivery.

For many years, Dr. Chesley lectured at the Exeter Nurses Training School based at Exeter Hospital. Her specialty was hygiene. In 1933, at the age of seventy-one, she surprised everyone by marrying George Lamprey, a local real estate broker and farmer. For their honeymoon, the couple took a car trip up the coast of Maine. She returned to practice after the trip and continued to serve the Exeter community until her death in 1941.

Today, the AMA states that 26 percent of all American physicians are women, although there are currently slightly more women than men in medical school. As rigorous as the training may be today, it must have been tougher in Alice Chesley's time, when not only was one judged by achievement but also gender.

THE CHESTNUT STREET JAIL

In the collection of the Exeter Historical Society there is a heavy key labeled, "Key of the old Exeter Jail." The origins of this key are somewhat uncertain. It was donated to the society in 1971 without any mention of how it was obtained by the donor. It is probably the same key referred to by Dr. William G. Perry, which he spotted once in an exhibit in Boston: "I went in and was much interested in the display which included all sorts of burglars' implements, photographs of notorious criminals and among other things a huge key labeled 'Key of the old Exeter jail.'"

Perry must have encountered the key in the late nineteenth century, and at that time Exeter had only one "old jail," the one that had been located on Chestnut Street. The key is remarkable not only for its size—it is a full five inches long—but also for the bludgeon attached as a fob. At 13.3 ounces, it would have settled all but the most difficult of prisoners. However, few criminals would have bothered scuffling with the jail keeper. It was far easier to just wait until one was locked in the cell. You see, Exeter's jail was notorious for its jailbreaks.

If Exeter had a jail in its infancy, there is no trace of it now. The earliest records mention the stocks and whipping post in front of the town house. This seems to have been sufficient to keep the population relatively honest for the first hundred or so years of the town's existence. By 1770, however, it was deemed necessary to build a jail in the newly organized county. Exeter, as the county seat, was chosen as the location and a parcel of land on the eastern bank of the river was purchased. Perry described the building as

two stories and of wood. The windows were small, with heavy iron bars. The doors of the cells were of oak, some four or five inches thick, studded with iron bolts; at the side was a small opening for the passage of food. In comparison with modern jails it was uncomfortable to say the least.

The "key of the old Exeter jail." Weighing in at almost a pound, the fob was the most useful law enforcement tool in the jail, which was well known for jailbreaks.

Local legend states that the first prisoner incarcerated in the new jail was the builder—for debt. In fact, most of the jail's inmates were there for nonpayment of debt. Under the watch of jail keeper Freese Dearborn, there were a total of 1,054 commitments to the jail from 1810 to 1831. Of these inmates, 730 were serving time for debt. The remaining 324 (of which 16 were female) were in for criminal offences. Of these, 20 escaped.

Escape seems to have always been an option for the inmates. During the Revolution, Exeter's jail was home to a number of Dutch Tories from New York State. One of them cleverly escaped with the aid of his wife. According to accounts, the lady went in to see her husband and returned a short time later with her bonnet pulled low and her muff drawn up to her face. By the time the alarm was sounded, "she" had already crossed the Great Bridge to the swamp and eventually made it to New Brunswick. Most of the New York Tories were boarded out to local families after paying a bond. The town needed its jail to contain its own homegrown loyalists.

By 1857, the jail—with its seemingly semipermeable timber walls and close location to the river and therefore the outside world—was deemed too small and not strong enough to contain its inmates. A new brick jail was built on Forest Street to house county prisoners until 1910.

SCANDAL IN EXETER, 1873

When Nathaniel Appleton Shute failed to return from his usual overnight business trip to Boston one January day in 1873, no one was particularly alarmed at first. Shute, the cashier of Granite State Bank in Exeter and treasurer of the Exeter Bank, often delayed his travels when urgent business came up. Besides his banking positions, Shute also traded stocks and bonds in the railroad industry. The three occupations combined gave him an estimated yearly income of over $3,000—quite comfortable for the time. Both he and his father were well-respected citizens of Exeter. Three days after the routine trip to Boston, however, Shute had still not returned home and his strange disappearance was noted in the *Exeter News-Letter*: "his unexplained absence caused much anxiety, and on Thursday morning a gentleman from this town proceeded to Boston to learn the cause of his absence, if possible. He ascertained that Mr. Shute had probably not been in Boston at all."

What Benjamin Merrill, a local wool merchant, had discovered was that Shute had fled town after embezzling nearly $150,000 from the two banks. In an era before banks were insured, the crime was both shocking and distressing to local citizens. The Exeter Bank immediately shut down all transactions until the damage could be appraised. But far worse than any monetary losses was the loss of trust in a man most people considered upright and honorable.

Shute had been born in Fitchburg, Massachusetts, in 1833, moving to Exeter with his family as a boy. His father was a carriage maker—a skilled craftsman of the time. Educated at Phillips Exeter Academy, young Shute went into the banking business in town, securing the position of cashier, or chief financial officer, while still a young man. He was brought up well and honestly by his parents and married Ellen Holbrook, with whom he had two

The Granite State Bank on Front Street.

daughters. By all accounts, he was well respected and highly trustworthy. To secure his positions as cashier and treasurer, his father, uncles and many local citizens signed bonds of security. All of these bonds later had to be paid by the disbelieving signees after Shute fled the country. Shute's aged father, dishonored and ashamed by his son's actions, was left to go through his papers and figure out what had driven him to such an act.

Perhaps his wife knew something was amiss. Two years earlier, Shute had unexpectedly sold his fine house on Pine Street for a mere $5,000. In early 1873, just before the crime, he presented her with $100 and told her to make the most of it for the year for they were now poor. The $5,000 was "lost." He was acting oddly that January. Usually a purchaser of a season pass on the Boston and Maine Railroad, Shute instead began buying single tickets for his business trips. Further investigations revealed that Shute's stock speculations were unsuccessful and he had fallen into the age-old gambler's fallacy, believing that the next big one would bail him out. By November of 1872, Shute was down over $42,000. Desperate and seeing no way out, he began to plan his crime. It is to his credit that he stole no personal savings, only bonds and investments. Anecdotes drifted into the newspapers of individuals who had entrusted their savings to Shute and feared they were lost, only to discover that he had faithfully taken care of the transaction before disappearing from town.

Nathaniel Appleton Shute, an Exeter bank cashier, embezzled nearly $150,000 from two area banks in 1873, an era before banks were insured.

Shute was later sighted in Cuba, but was never brought back to Exeter to stand trial. Both banks weathered the loss of funds. Shute's little daughters fared well—his younger daughter, Mary, who was only eight when her father abandoned the family, became an instructor of Greek at Smith College and later did graduate work in archaeology at Yale and Gottingen University. His wife never seemed to recover from the shock of her husband's crime. She died in 1881 at the age of forty-four. Shute himself made occasional contact with his father through untraceable letters. He died on April Fool's Day 1900, in Bournemouth, England—a testament to the foolishness of imprudent speculation.

THE BRICKYARD RIOT
OF 1891

As the summer of 1891 drew to a close, the quiet pace of life in Exeter was interrupted by a violent labor dispute and simmering ethnic tensions. The Wiggin and Clark Brickyard was located near the railroad tracks beyond Forest Street in a part of town known for its working-class neighborhood. The town jail had been relocated to the area in part because of its relative isolation. Although it received little attention, it was the oldest part of Exeter, and much later the Daughters of the American Revolution would put up a monument marking its historic importance as the site of the first meetinghouse.

There had been brickyards in the area for decades, but by the late nineteenth century, homegrown labor was hard to come by. Brick making was heavy, hard work. First the clay had to be plowed out of the ground and mixed with water and gravel. The mixture was then thrown into wooden molds and set out to dry. After drying, the bricks were stacked for firing; all of this heavy hauling was done by hired laborers.

Between 1876 and the turn of the century, there was an influx of Italian immigrants coming to America. Unlike other immigrants, this group intended to work for a few years and return home. They didn't set down roots, instead gravitating toward manual labor jobs like road building or seasonal work that would allow them to return to Italy during the colder months. Wiggin and Clark hired laborers for the brick-making season, the contracts most likely brokered by a third party.

The boss of the yard was a French Canadian named John Dugay. Whether the Italian workers resented him for his heritage or his manner has never been fully explained, but on the morning of August 19, Antoni Bubba pulled out a sharpened blade (either a razor or a stiletto, depending on which source you pick) and threatened Dugay, who, claiming not to know

Exeter Police Department in the town hall station around 1900. Police were not routinely armed when on duty.

the provocation, raced into town and had a warrant sworn out for Bubba's arrest. Officer Edmund Thurston arrived a short time later, armed with only a billy club and an arrest warrant to take the offender into custody. As he was handcuffing Bubba, three other Italian laborers attacked him with clubs, beating him senseless. They then roughed up Dugay and several other yard workers before chasing them into the woods. The town alarm was sounded and scores of firefighters and townsfolk quickly gathered to pursue the "rioters." Thurston was rescued by two prisoners who had been working in the nearby jail yard. They carried him back to the jail, where a doctor quickly arrived to tend his wounds. Dugay ran down Newmarket Road shouting, "Murder! Murder!" but participated little in the pursuit of the criminals.

Bubba, Vincenzo Nesci and Giovanni and Domenico Conati were overtaken hours later in Plaistow. A week later, at a hearing in the Exeter Court, more of the story came out. Speaking through an interpreter, the men described their aggravation with the brickyard's management and

The Forest Street Jail, located just south of the Wiggin and Clark Brickyard.

what they felt was unfair pay practices. The brickyard insisted that the men were fully informed that they would be paid at the end of the season—later that fall—and it had been agreed that they would receive board and small allotments until that time. John Templeton observed in the *Exeter News-Letter*: "While the Italians' attack upon Officer Thurston was unprovoked and universally condemned, the fact is patent that they are none the less objects of a considerable measure of sympathy." It's worth noting that while they were locked in the town jail, "they were highly pleased with their improved boarding place." Apparently the jail provided better lodging and food than that provided by the brickyard.

Officer Thurston recovered and the trial was held in October, all the men changed their pleas to guilty and received thirty days time served. Considering the headline of "Deadly Assault" and the excitement that briefly erupted, the Brickyard Riot of 1891 ended quietly.

CRIME OF PASSION

As he lay bleeding from a self-inflicted wound after shooting his love in an adjoining room, Charles Tash was asked if he regretted what he had done. "He answered," reported the *Exeter News-Letter*, that "he was sorry that Sally suffered so much pain—he had intended that both should die without pain." Sally Moore, who had been on the receiving end of Tash's affections for over two years, had refused to marry him because her friends would object to her wedding a man of color. Yet it may have been his color that saved him from the gallows.

Charles Tash was the son of Oxford Tash, who had earned his freedom fighting in the American Revolution. After the war, Tash moved to Exeter, where he joined the growing community of free black war pensioners. The Tash family was well respected in town, even if their "degraded caste" kept them at the bottom of the economic ladder. All accounts of Charles describe a man of unquestionable high character: "excellent manners and high-spirited"; "a gentleman"; and "possessed of some property, intelligent, and well-educated, his moral character and general habits have always been exemplary." A note to the *News-Letter* shortly after the shooting said of Tash: "He is temperate, industrious, and respectful in his demeanor, and received that notice and respect in return from *all* who knew him." It seemed that no one in town was willing to speak badly of Charles Tash. At the trial, held in December of 1831, the prosecution conceded that "his general character until the time of committing this act, had been irreproachable, and that his disposition was peaceful and mild."

A few months before the shooting, Tash had approached Moore with his proposal and she refused him. She didn't seem to object to him personally, nor did her family. Tash asserted that it was her friends who encouraged her to break off the relationship. He became so despondent that his housekeeper called Doctor Perry. Perry found Tash to be depressed, but believed he would recover. In spite of his sad demeanor, Tash continued his everyday tasks and was offered a job. Commodore Long was sailing on a two-year cruise and needed a reliable steward. It seemed like just the thing to snap him out of his moodiness. The night before he was to set sail, Tash decided to ask Sally one more time if she would have him. He spoke to her in the late afternoon and the two agreed to meet later at her mother's house on Cass Street. Tash arrived and visited with the family for over an hour before Sally's mother and brother retired for the night. According to the court records, they talked of many subjects and he did not appear to be uneasy in any way. But he had brought two loaded pistols with him and when Sally alighted the stairs to go to bed, he fired, hitting her in the abdomen. As he ran through the stairwell toward the back of the house, he turned the other pistol on himself, but misfired and the bullets hit his arm. Although Sally was not expected to survive, both she and Tash recovered.

At the trial, his defense team pleaded "insanity"—a difficult thing to prove given that everyone in town considered Tash to be such a stable and reliable person. But the defense had another card to play—Tash's very "degraded state" ("race" was never used) made his unrequited love all the more unobtainable. His lawyer, Ichabod Bartlett, stated

> *He could never think of wrestling for power, glory, or distinction—his color was an insuperable bar to the attainment of such objects. But when he had obtained the affection of a young woman of a color different from his own, his whole mind was centered there. Yet he met with unexpected obstacles— not from the young woman herself, but from her surrounding friends. This was a tremendous shock, and the natural, perhaps inevitable consequence would be mental delusion.*

The prosecution would have nothing of the strange defense, instructing the jury: "Notwithstanding the African hue of his complexion, there is no danger of prejudices being entertained against the prisoner. You will be more likely to be biased in his favor. You may consider him a friendless and degraded black and sympathize with him. But it is your duty to be impartial, to lean the other way."

The conflicted jury, sensitive to the growing abolitionism in town yet skeptical of the temporary insanity defense, brought in a verdict of guilty, but under peculiar circumstances. Tash never served any more time. He

Here at 25 Cass Street in 1831, a lovesick Charles Tash tried to murder Sally Moore and commit suicide so they would be together for eternity. His attempt failed—both he and Sally survived, and Tash faced charges for attempted murder. The fact that he was black and Sally white factored into the case, ultimately working in Tash's favor.

was remanded into his own custody and eventually received a respite on account of unsoundness of mind. Even the judge, it seemed, was unwilling to punish a man of respectable character for a crime of love.

Temperance and the New Englander

It always puzzled me, when studying geography, that we live in a temperate zone. "Temperate" means free from extremes—a hard definition for a child who has just waited in subzero temperatures for the school bus to fully grasp. Once freed from school for the summer, that same child might reflect once again upon "temperate" while trudging through the heat to the YMCA camp bus. Who wrote this crazy definition anyway?

It doesn't help us that the temperance movement that took shape in the early 1800s wasn't at all about temperate drinking. A temperate drinker would imbibe a bit and stop before too much alcohol had taken effect. By the mid-1800s, however, "temperance" was viewed as "abstinence," and the movement became entwined with other movements, most particularly the women's rights movement, and unfortunately also with the nativist movement.

The earliest Europeans to arrive in New Hampshire had no complicated issues with alcohol. Indeed, ale, wine and rum were considered much safer to drink than the local water. Every housewife was a capable brewer, often mixing her ale in the same wooden trough she used to make the family's bread. Yeast was women's domain, and their mastery of it spoke volumes about their worth. Although the early settlers drank a great deal (and our records from John Gidding's accounts attest that rum was his highest-selling commodity), drunkenness was considered a sin akin to gluttony. The drink wasn't to blame; the overindulgence was. Most town meetings and court sessions in early New England broke often for refreshments in the local tavern. Kind of makes you want to go back to the old town meeting system, doesn't it?

After the American Revolution, however, taverns began to fill with idlers, and drunkenness became more of a social problem. Perhaps a strong drink

Although it may look like Harold McKeen is about to offer you a drink at the Folsom Tavern in 1907, it would have had to be lemonade because Exeter townspeople voted the town dry in 1904.

didn't really strengthen the muscles after all. The stirrings of the temperance movement began in the late eighteenth century. In its early days, it meant just what the name implies—temperance—our schoolchild's understanding of no extremes. Drink would be tolerated if not abused, and it is this time period from which we derive the name for the movement. During the mid-nineteenth century, though, temperance organizers had begun to encourage people (read: men, for women drank more discretely from patent medicines that were concocted primarily of alcohol with an occasional opium kicker) to take "the pledge." The temperance pledge was actually an abstinence pledge, with those adherents vowing never to take any strong drink at all. Why all the fuss when responsible drinking might be easier to achieve? There are a number of reasons the temperance movement gained momentum. The women's suffrage movement became very active after the Civil War. During a time when women had no political rights and fewer civil rights, the movement took aim at abuses perpetuated on women. The social ills of men drinking away the family wages were front and center in the eyes of many. The stereotype of the husband arriving home on payday, drunk and abusive, beating his wife and children and leaving the larder empty for another week became an icon in the public's mind. Add to this a hefty fear of European immigrants—not the English-speaking, white, Protestant type, of course, but the foreign-tongued, beer-drinking Catholic type—and you have good reason to shut down the saloons.

Maine passed statewide prohibition in 1847 and was viewed as a model for temperance workers in other states. As the states passed their own prohibitive laws, however, their court systems consistently threw them out as unconstitutional. New Hampshire passed legislation in 1903 allowing local communities to decide whether to license establishments for the sale of liquor. In Exeter, it led to lively debate every two years when the licensing laws had to be voted on. The votes were always close, but Exeter remained officially dry, although police records indicate there was only varying success with enforcement. Oddly, although there were high numbers of arrests for drunkenness in the 1910s, the numbers dropped suddenly just before national prohibition was passed in 1920. To proponents of prohibition, the national law would finally bring an end to the circus-like atmosphere of town meetings every two years. It didn't, however, bring an end to drinking in the town. Once prohibition was passed, arrests for drunkenness and intoxication rose steadily and reached pre-licensing rates within five years. The numbers never went down again.

Beer became legal again in early 1933 after Franklin Roosevelt had the prohibition regulations slightly rewritten to exclude 3 percent alcohol content. After the repeal of the Eighteenth Amendment later that year, local control was again restored. The 1934 election saw the prohibitionists lose in a vote of 865 to 840. Exeter's first state liquor store was opened in 1935. Historian Nancy Merrill commented, "That there was still some feeling about the sale of liquor in town was attested to by those who departed from the store carrying their brown paper bags under their coats."

THE ANTI-SUFFRAGETTES

One of the heroes of the Exeter Historical Society would have to be Frances Perry Dudley. She was one of the founders of the society and a tireless worker for many social causes in the early twentieth century. She was concerned about the lives and health of the people of Exeter and New Hampshire, particularly the many working people in the town. Like wealthy club women across the country, she was profoundly influenced by the progressive movement and saw it as her duty to uplift the social and moral standards of the day. Often overlooked in her biography was her tireless effort to *prevent* what was viewed as a destroyer of the social order—women's suffrage.

The idea of allowing women to vote had been knocking around for nearly one hundred years before it became one of the most controversial issues of the early twentieth century. Like marriage laws, voting regulations are considered part of the reserved rights of individual states. A few western states had allowed women the right to vote, but depending on how you looked at it, it had either been a great success or a great failure. Supporters of women's suffrage, often coming from the temperance movement, had argued that women's votes would cure many social ills—child labor, public drunkenness, poverty—because women were naturally more nurturing and would vote for the public good. Warfare would end because the influence of the gentler sex would prevent belligerent legislation. None of these outcomes had occurred in the states where women routinely cast votes; however, it would have proven difficult to revoke voting rights once half the population didn't want to give it up. So, the "western experiment" sat amid the controversy unable to prove or disprove positive changes in society except that women, once given the right to vote, were reluctant to the point of militancy to give it up.

So the extension of this experiment had to be stopped before society fell apart utterly. In 1911, the National Association Opposed to Women's Suffrage was formed and the New Hampshire Association Opposed to Women's Suffrage quickly followed. The president of this statewide organization was our own Frances Perry Dudley. Organized and run entirely by women, the group, almost entirely made up of wealthy, well-educated wives of New Hampshire's upper crust, sought to prevent the defeminization of American women. The well-meaning women—none of whom worked for wages or had to support families—believed strongly that politics was the realm of men. Women led by example, not by legislation. Should the terrible Twentieth Amendment pass, men and women would be viewed as social equals and the deference women enjoyed by being above such messy matters would be taken away.

As the national amendment loomed, opposing meetings were held throughout the state. The suffragettes would hold a rally and the "antis" would hold a public meeting. Dueling editorials appeared in the *Exeter News-Letter*. After sixteen-year-old Helen Tufts attended one such meeting in 1912

Thursday, May 16, 1912

Diary entry of Helen Tufts, May 16, 1912, after she returned from an anti-suffrage speech.

with her mother, Effie—an ardent member of the anti-suffrage movement—Helen noted in her diary: "Went to Town Hall with Mother to hear two ladies speak on anti-suffrage. Very Good [underlined three times]. I'm an 'anti.'" One of the speakers, Mrs. A.J. George of Boston, convincingly argued that "women's suffrage would only increase the proportion of irresponsible voters." She stated that voting rights and the payment of property taxes have no connection since few women owned property. Of course, those who do are required to pay taxes, but this is the minority of women.

The biggest argument against extending suffrage was that it would cause the breakdown of the family, as women by their nature would vote differently from men; it followed that marriages would become politically tense and divorce rates would skyrocket.

Frances Perry Dudley (credited, of course, as "Mrs. A.T. Dudley") published a letter written by Miss Elizabeth Parker that opined:

> *Suffrage would not be voluntary; it would be a duty, and we think also a burden. We feel that women are today doing their fair share of the world's*

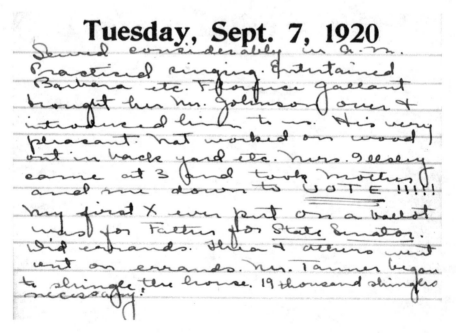

Diary entry of Helen Tufts, September 7, 1920, the day she cast her first ballot.

work, and we ask that until we have in some measure covered the fields for which we are specially well adapted, we be not required to undertake work for which we have no peculiar fitness, and which would, moreover, hamper seriously our usefulness in our present endeavors.

You see, the anti-suffragists were simply trying to protect women from the overwhelming burden of political life. Lost on them entirely was that they had become politicized in order to achieve this goal.

Alas, for the anti-suffrage forces, the Twentieth Amendment to the constitution fell to the suffragettes. Helen Tufts's father, James Tufts, a state senator, did his best to oppose the measure. On September 10, 1919, she wrote: "Father fought it, spoke etc, but N.H. passed the suffrage amendment 18 to 10. Worse Luck!" The defeat stung so badly that many women refused to vote. Well, not really. The following year on September 7, Helen Tufts, now nearly twenty-four, cast her first vote in the primary elections and proudly wrote in her diary: "Mrs. Illsley came at 3 and took Mother and me down to VOTE!!! My first X ever put on a ballot was for Father for State Senator." The man who had opposed her right to vote won in the subsequent election. The genie was out of the bottle and society has been in decline ever since.

THE LADIES OF THE
FRAUENVEREIN

In the years following the Civil War, middle-class American women enjoyed an increase in leisure time that had never existed before. Labor-saving devices, like the carpet sweeper and iron cook stove, combined with income levels that allowed for hired help, provided them with a measure of freedom from domestic chores. What to do with all that spare time—there are only so many doilies one can make. Denied the right to vote at this time, women began to pursue other intellectual outlets.

In many parts of the country, women's groups organized both formally and informally. Some had a stated purpose, such as the Ladies Relief Corps, an auxiliary group attached to the Grand Army of the Republic, which provided support to Civil War veterans and widows. Other groups formed as study clubs and reading circles. One such club, formed in 1868 in New York City was called Sorosis, a name derived from Greek as either "fruit formed of many flowers" or a reference to sisterhood. The women of Sorosis met weekly to further the educational and social activities of women. The group had initially formed in a haughty response to being shut out of a lecture featuring Charles Dickens simply because it was held at a men's club.

Cosmopolitan women may have been a bit uppity to start their own club, but even here in Exeter there was a small, but growing, group of middle-class women eager to broaden their intellectual life and get away from the house for a few hours. A small group of ladies gathered to form just such a group, calling themselves Frauenverein—German for "Women's Association." According to Mrs. George Cross (her real name was "Mary," but it would never have appeared publically as such—women's names were somehow considered unladylike for married women): "In the autumn of 1884 a few ladies were wont to meet together one afternoon each week in some one of their parlors to study Byron's *Childe Harold*." This lengthy poem followed

The Ladies of the Frauenverein photographed in Miss Annie Chadwick's garden on May 23, 1889.

the travels of a young man as he searched for meaning in an often-frivolous world. The ladies of Frauenverein studied the poem for months, stopping only for tea and other light refreshments. In January of the following year, they held a more formal meeting to celebrate Lord Byron's birthday. Miss Annie Chadwick composed a poem of her own for the occasion:

We pause today that we may not forget
The genius, to whom thanks are due
For many things, which ne'er before we knew
We'd like to have him here today,
Perhaps 'tis well though, that he's far away
For though we all are nice and neat
We know he'd hate us if he saw us eat!

The group quickly doubled in size, from the original nine to eighteen members. After they had put Byron to bed, they began to study all things German—the geography, the culture, the myths, the music, all infused with heavy doses of tea, cakes and lively discussion. After Germany, they moved on to Italy and later the British Isles. Individual members would serve as speakers for the event. Although the club was for women only, occasionally men were allowed to attend special meetings. "I am sure that the gentlemen who partook of the charming tea given one May evening at Mrs. Bell's will say that the ladies have not pursued their literary labors to the neglect of domestic accomplishments," Mrs. Cross felt compelled to comment, lest those newly bulging brains got in the way of the stove. The group was still active in 1918 when, in a fit of World War I patriotism, they changed the name to Friday Club, so it wouldn't sound so German.

It's not fair to mock the sincerity of these women. After all, Frauenverein women are not at all unlike most book club women of today. One of my friends, when asked to join a committee, replied that she would do so only if we changed the regular meeting date. She was in a book club, you see. "Five women and a bottle of wine talking about books—you don't mess with that," she said.

George Washington
Stepped Here

A hhh, President's Day. For the most part, modern observances of this holiday give us a day off school and a boost in car sales. At our house, we ritually have a cherry pie in memory of George Washington—never mind that he probably never cut down his father's cherry tree or that my kids don't even like cherry pie. I still feel the need to mark the day with some semblance of ritual.

Perhaps in the future, we could remember George Washington's triumphant visit to Exeter in 1789. Of course, we'd have to move our celebration to the fall. In mid-October of 1789, the newly inaugurated president left his mansion in New York City and embarked on a tour of New England. Ignoring Rhode Island, which hadn't yet adopted the Constitution, Washington rode through Connecticut to Boston, arriving at the New Hampshire border on October 31. After a few fun-filled days spent in Portsmouth, which we aren't interested in, Washington set out for Exeter punctually at 7:30 a.m. on November 4. Perhaps having overindulged in Portsmouth's attention and adulation, the president requested a quiet departure and rode on horseback rather than in his carriage. By the time he passed through Stratham, however, the roads were packed with well-wishers. Everyone knew the president was on his way, except the fine citizens of Exeter, who weren't quite prepared for his arrival.

Washington rode into town at 10:00 a.m. and was greeted by a flurry of activity. A planned cavalcade of dignitaries failed to collect on time and it was left to Captain Simon Wiggin and his artillery company to greet the president with a thirteen-gun salute. Washington, to his credit, seemed not to notice our lack of decorum and made no mention of it in his diary or letters. Instead, he politely dismounted and availed himself of breakfast at the public house kept by Colonel Samuel Folsom—the very same Folsom's Tavern that

George Washington never slept here, but he did stop for breakfast on the morning of November 4, 1789, on a visit that was not related to a presidential primary.

has lately been seen wandering around town. Its original location was on the corner of Front and Water Streets. No one bothered to record what the president ate—I've always imagined alewives and cherry pie—but we do know he was waited upon by Colonel Nicholas Gilman and seventeen-year-old Margaret Emery. Margaret was the sister-in-law of Samuel Folsom, the innkeeper. By most accounts, she "insisted" on waiting on the president and was rewarded for her efforts by a few kind words and a kiss, which conferred celebrity status on the young woman for life. He was invited to stay for the day and even the night, but he had already made commitments farther down the road.

The residents gave him a grand send-off, complete with the tardy cavalcade planned for his arrival. Our attachment to the great president has never dimmed—although it has always been tempered with our practical, New England sentimentality. Elizabeth Dow Leonard wrote:

Historically Speaking

It was said that when news of General Washington's death was announced in Exeter, many ladies thought it necessary to faint, Mrs. Tenney among the number. She had a valuable mirror in her hand when she received the terrible news of G.W.'s fate. She walked leisurely across the room, laid the mirror safely down, placed herself in the proper attitude, adjusted her garments like Caesar when he fell, and then fainted away, and so paid her patriotic tribute to the great man's memory and did not sacrifice her looking glass, as a less sensible and discreet woman would have done.

Robert Todd Lincoln's
Big Flunk

When Abraham Lincoln's son, Robert Todd Lincoln, traveled to Cambridge in 1859 to attend Harvard, he thought he was well prepared for admission. But even the letter of introduction from Stephen Douglas, his father's opponent in the Illinois senate race, wasn't enough to overcome the fact that young Robert had flunked his admission exams. His failure surprised him, although he later commented that his earlier attendance at Illinois State University—a prep school, not really a university—was so lax in academics that "we did just what pleased us, study consuming only a very small portion of our time." It was suggested that he attend a more formal school and in due course, young Robert was enrolled in a yearlong cramming session at Phillips Exeter Academy under the watchful eye of Principal Gideon Soule.

Most academy students at this time boarded at Abbott Hall on the campus grounds, but Robert Lincoln, with the help of his father's friend, Amos Tuck, secured a room in the boardinghouse of Mrs. S.B. Clark in the Folsom Block on Pleasant Street. Here he shared a room with his friend George Latham. Robert's father promised to visit him as soon as family finances would allow. Bob hunkered down with his books, studying the required Latin, Greek, mathematics, composition and declamation. Although the academy lost most of its records in a series of fires, Lincoln's classmate, B. Judson Perkins, recorded the grades of the entire class of 1860 in his diary. Sixteen-year-old Lincoln passed the year with a very respectable 93 average, in the top half of his class.

In the winter of his year at Exeter, Robert received the news that his father would be coming east. Lincoln had been offered the tidy sum of $200 to speak at the Cooper Institute in New York City. The speaking fee would more than pay for travel expenses. Lincoln bought himself a new suit, packed

The Folsom Block on the corner of Pleasant and Water Streets. Robert Todd Lincoln roomed in this house, then run by Mrs. Clark, during his time at Phillips Exeter Academy (1859–60). Abraham Lincoln came to visit his son and possibly stayed in Robert's room.

a few things and knocked the crowd dead in New York. When local political leaders found out he was planning to visit Robert in Exeter, he was quickly inundated with requests to speak throughout the state. The request from Dover was addressed to "————Lincoln, son of Abraham Lincoln, Exeter, NH." The Republican Party leader of that town didn't even know Robert's first name. Polite, as always, Robert answered that he would have his father reply as soon as he arrived.

The elder Lincoln arrived in Exeter on the late afternoon train on Wednesday, February 29. Between his speaking engagements in New Hampshire, Lincoln would spend three nights in Exeter, although there are four places in town that lay claim to housing him. Most of his time was spent with Robert and his friends, although he did agree to address the town on March 3 at the relatively new town hall. There is no record of what Lincoln said at that meeting, but many people remembered the evening. Marshall Snow, another classmate of Robert's, recalled years later: "We sat and stared at Mr. Lincoln. We whispered to each other: 'Isn't it too bad Bob's father is so homely? Don't you feel sorry for him?'" Lincoln won over the crowd, as he had in New York, and Snow commented that when he spoke, "His face lighted up and the man was changed. There was no more pity for our friend Bob; we were proud of his father, and when the exercises of the evening were over and the opportunity was offered to those who desired to meet Mr. Lincoln, we were the first to mount the platform and grasp him by the hand."

The next morning, Lincoln, not a regular churchgoer, attended services at the Second Parish Church to accommodate Robert's academy-imposed compulsory attendance. The pew he sat in is still preserved. His visit ended all too soon that evening, but many have credited the trip east with launching his presidential campaign. Robert called it his "greatest flunk."

Years later, in 1918, former president William Howard Taft visited Exeter and was introduced by Exeter Academy Professor James Arthur Tufts, who noted that Taft didn't need to send his son to school at Exeter to get elected. Tufts's daughter, Helen, noted in her diary that "Mr. T chuckled and said he wished he had known about that way of getting elected and he might have sent Charlie here before his second trial for election!"

PRESIDENTIAL VISIT, SUMMER OF 1889

Just about everyone in Exeter knows that George Washington visited the town in 1789. It was part of his presidential visit to see the New England states. Prior to the 1950s, when New Hampshire became the Primary State that it is today, few candidates made their way to Exeter. And let's face it, once the primary is over and the endless parade of candidates has packed up, the winners don't return. Maybe that's why we hold Washington's visit in such high regard. He was already elected when he stopped by to check up on us. It was like a phone call from Dad: "How are you doing? How's the weather down there? Don't forget to get your oil changed. Bye, now."

In the summer of 1889, excitement was high in expectation of another rare presidential visit. Benjamin Harrison, on his way to Bar Harbor, Maine, was due to stop briefly at the Exeter depot on Lincoln Street. Harrison is one of those easily forgotten one-term presidents, the bologna in the Grover Cleveland sandwich. During an era when machine politics could put modern lobbyists to shame, he managed to defeat the incumbent Cleveland by losing the popular vote but winning the Electoral College. Cleveland would fight back in the next election, much to the dismay of Exeter's Republicans.

Harrison was a protectionist and believed in high tariffs, supporting the McKinley Tariff Act that ultimately led to the disastrous economic depression of the 1890s. But he also saw six new states admitted to the Union—Montana, Idaho, Washington, Wyoming and the Dakotas. Like two squabbling twins, North and South Dakota each wanted to be granted statehood before the other. Harrison decided the issue by covering the bills, shuffling them and then signing them quickly without ever knowing which came first.

There are two accounts of Harrison's visit to Exeter. The *Exeter News-Letter* reported that "the presidential train drew into the station at Exeter

President Benjamin Harrison.

at fourteen minutes past ten. Citizens of Exeter and neighboring towns, irrespective of party and including many ladies, crowded the platforms. Twelve hundred would be a moderate estimate of their number, and good judges set it at fifteen hundred." The *Exeter Gazette*, however, was less caught up with specifics. "Shortly after 10 o'clock the special train bearing the

President arrived at the depot where a crowd numbering several hundred was awaiting his arrival. As soon as it came to a standstill a rush was made for the end of the rear car where the President was discovered standing on the platform."

At this point, the two reporters (most likely John Templeton of the *News-Letter*, and James Wingate of the *Gazette*) tell similar tales. Templeton: "Men swarmed upon the track and surged towards the train until they could grasp the President by the hand. Ladies and children crowded upon the car steps for the same purpose." Wingate: "The President stood there shaking hands with the crowd who surged around him in the desire to seize his hand. There were quite a number of ladies among the number who had the pleasure of shaking hands with the Chief Magistrate."

Both mentioned the ladies as if surprised that women could be interested in the president. Politics were, after all, part of the messy world that was owned by men. The ladies had no more say in government than the children. Perhaps they were attracted to the outfit the president was wearing. The *News-Letter* wasn't particularly impressed: "The President wore a suit of drab,

Townspeople, "irrespective of party," turned out in large numbers to catch a glimpse of the president at the Lincoln Street Depot.

the Prince Albert coat closely buttoned." The *Gazette* could hardly contain itself: "The President, who was bare-headed, wore a neat fitting gray Prince Albert suit and a black four-in-hand tie."

The whole event was over quickly. The *News-Letter*, in its typically careful way, summed up the visit: "The train remained in Exeter seven minutes." "After a stop of about fifteen minutes the train proceeded on its way," responded the *Gazette*.

Whether he was well dressed or in "drab," stayed for seven minutes or fifteen, the president's visit excited the town to a degree not felt since James K. Polk stopped by thirty years earlier. A few other sitting presidents would visit—Theodore Roosevelt, Harry Truman and Gerald Ford—but they were here for campaign purposes and Roosevelt's train didn't even stop, it just slowed down at the depot. Harrison may not have stepped off the train, but at least he had the courtesy to stop.

WAR OF 1812

A t one time, January 8 was practically a national holiday. Everywhere across the United States flags were flown and parades were held to celebrate our great victory over the British at the Battle of New Orleans in 1815. Everywhere except in New England. Charles Bell, Exeter's former governor and official historian, devotes just three sentences of commentary about the war in his *History of Exeter, New Hampshire*, written in 1888. He then lists the Exeter men who reluctantly joined the militia to defend the seacoast communities.

We tend to think of the Vietnam War as the most divisive conflict in U.S. history, but the War of 1812 almost prompted New England to secede from the Union. Had he spent more time discussing the war, Bell would have had quite a tale to tell about politics, economics and questions of patriotism, but instead he simply dropped the war from his narrative, dismissing it as unpopular. "With the party which brought on the war with Great Britain in 1812, the people of Exeter, in common with the majority of those of New England, had little sympathy. It was not to be expected, therefore, that they would be ready to volunteer, to any extent, to serve in the army in that contest."

In a nutshell, there were two political parties in the United States in 1812—the Federalists and the Democratic-Republicans—and both had old scores to settle. The Federalists were still loyal to Great Britain because of our common heritage and language, even though we'd just finished fighting the Revolution a few years before. Democratic-Republicans, on the other hand, still felt grateful to the French for helping us beat the British. And in 1812, Britain and France were at war with one another. The fledgling United States found neutrality a bit difficult to maintain at times, particularly when the Northeast was firmly Federalist while the government in Washington had

Governor John Taylor Gilman, a Federalist from Exeter, was elected in 1813. In his inaugural remarks, he was unable to hide his contempt for the administration of President Madison and the policies that led to the War of 1812.

become Democratic-Republican. New Englanders were rightly concerned that war with Britain would disrupt trade, and President Madison's crazy plan to attack Canada and use it as a bargaining chip to end British abuses didn't sit well. Early on, the *Constitutionalist*, printed in Exeter, editorialized that "we are far from applauding or even upholding the wicked measures of an unwise administration. It is believed, that not one in ten of the citizens of New-England and New-York, if now called upon to express their unbiased opinion, would approve the War."

John Taylor Gilman, a Federalist from Exeter, was elected as governor of New Hampshire during the war. His inaugural remarks made his stand perfectly clear: "It is not doubted that we have had great causes of complaint against both Great Britain and France, and perhaps at some former period much greater against one or both of these governments than existed against the British at the time of the declaration of war." The British, although stretched thin in resources, quickly blockaded most of the East Coast. Trade almost came to a standstill, except for illegal trade, which some New Englanders practiced with great enthusiasm. Honest merchants found it hard going and never really recovered after the war. Even those who might have profited from the war found it difficult to recoup losses. Exeter gunsmith Joshua Barstow signed a contract with the U.S. government to make twenty-

Musket made by Joshua Barstow for the War of 1812. Barstow was an Exeter gunsmith who contracted with the U.S. government to make 2,500 muskets. Due to mismanagement on the part of the government, the contract was never completed.

five hundred muskets over a five-year period for $10.75 each. The war should have made Barstow a wealthy man, but inefficiencies in government inspection and a string of bad checks from Uncle Sam forced him to sell many of his muskets to private citizens at a better price. The contract was never completed.

Although you wouldn't know it from Charles Bell, all was not quiet on the seacoast of New Hampshire. Beginning in 1814, British ships cruised along the coastline, menacing the citizenry as stories trickled down from as near as Castine, Maine, where the British had attacked. Fear was palpable in the region. Elizabeth Dow Leonard, who recalled her life as a child in Exeter during the war, recalled that people "had a chronic dread of English invasion. Every little while during the war would come more or less graphic and horrible accounts of the landing of the enemy at one of those out-of-the-way places, who were always coming directly to invade our quiet village, kill all the men and make prisoners of war of the women and children whom they did not eat on the spot!" Arrangements were made to quickly transport all the children out of town in the case of invasion and on June 21, 1814, it seemed the British had actually begun to land at Rye. Panic ensued in many seacoast towns. Leonard recalled, "Everything was in awful chaos. The alarm-bell was rung…the military putting on their cocked hats and loading their rusty muskets to defend their firesides, and we children promised to be transported in heavy wagons to places of safety, where they would hunt in vain to find us."

It proved to be a false alarm, the British having long before determined that New Hampshire was not a target. But the unpopular war had come awfully close. A convention was held in Hartford, Connecticut, in December to secretly discuss the possibility of withdrawing from the United States. Most of northern Maine had already sworn allegiance to Britain. But by that time, Britain had already tired of the fight and made diplomatic moves to formulate a cessation to hostilities. Indeed, the famed Battle of New Orleans—the only truly great land victory the United States had during the war—was fought after the peace treaty was signed. Maine was returned to the United States.

In spite of the fact that we didn't actually win the war—no territory was gained or lost—Americans were emboldened by Jackson's efforts at New Orleans enough to at least feel like the world now took us seriously. To Charles Bell, however, the war was still an embarrassment and a failure of diplomacy.

THE END OF THE
ESTABLISHED CHURCH

It might be hard to swallow, but New Hampshire (the "Live Free or Die" state) was one of the last states to legally sanction an established church system. Although New Hampshire was the first New England state to ratify the Constitution's First Amendment, guaranteeing freedom of religion, this doesn't seem to have been interpreted as anything that might affect the strong church/state ties on a local level. Indeed, most New Hampshire citizens believed that the Constitution guaranteed them the right to an established church. But let's back up and go over some history.

The earliest European settlers in New Hampshire were largely Puritan stock who had drifted in from the Massachusetts Bay Colony. In fact, the Massachusetts Bay Colony governed parts of New Hampshire for a number of years. Even in a place like Exeter, settled by dissenters of Puritan teachings, the basic civil structure followed that of the Massachusetts Bay Colony. Towns were formed around a meetinghouse, which served double duty as both a town hall and church. As such, it made perfect sense that the townspeople should support the church and its leader through annual taxes. Besides, if you legislated that everyone belonged to the town church, you could control the population a bit better from a moral standpoint. Everyone was the same Calvinistic, anti-papist, hopefully sanctified white Protestant—right? How could there possibly be any problems with such an ironclad system?

Unfortunately, we New Hampshire folks have been crotchety for centuries. Maybe it's the weather. In Exeter, the trouble began in 1743, when some members of the established church—and by this I mean the ancestors of our current Congregational Church—were drawn to a new revivalist style of preaching. The "New Lights" preached a message of grace with more emphasis on one's conversion experience. Unhappy with the orthodoxy being preached at the main church, they began to hold their own meetings.

Exeter's Second Parish Church stood on the grounds of Phillips Exeter Academy on Front Street. The congregation was a breakaway sect of the original—and legally sanctioned—First Parish Church. The two churches eventually settled their differences and reunited in 1920.

We were well beyond the days when one could be thrown in the stocks for not attending Sunday services, so this didn't bother anyone too terribly much. The real issue was that the newly formed "Second Parish Church" members still had to pay taxes through the town to support the First Parish and its minister. And as you can imagine, this kind of thing just made them crazy.

By 1800, the Baptist congregation had organized in town, followed shortly by the Methodists. By 1810, a small congregation of Universalists were, in the words of historian George Barstow, "compelled to pay for the erection of churches they never entered, for teachings they never heard, and clerical labors which they conscientiously regarded as tending only to perpetuate the dominion of religious errors over the public mind." The town would eventually allow one to pay the tax directly to the church of one's choice, but it was somewhat complicated to file all the paperwork and the tax assessment was still placed at a mandatory level. People who where indifferent to religious matters, or believed in a creed not affiliated with the local churches, were still forced to pay.

A disestablishment movement began to grow under the premise that it was necessary to stop sanctioning religion in order to allow religion to flourish. As was expected, the antidisestablishment camp argued that any such move would destroy religion and public morals. Convinced that the Constitution implied that "every man ought to be compelled to pay for the support of religion somewhere," many legislators were suspicious of the Toleration Act, as introduced by Governor Samuel Bell in 1819. But the established church had seen its day, and more liberal ideas prevailed. In spite of the "dangers of multiplying sects," the Toleration Act was passed and our places of worship became free from civil authority.

Contrary to the arguments, morals did not fall into a decline, nor did the churches find themselves empty on Sunday mornings. Church attendance increased, as did monetary support. It seems that New Hampshire folks were never opposed to religion—we just didn't take kindly to being told what to do with our money. Some things never change.

A DAY AT THE BEACH

In 1860, Exeter youth B. Judson Perkins decided to spend a day at Hampton Beach with his cousin. "Moses and I went to the beach today. Started at one o'clock arrived there at three, started on the return at eight. Had a very pleasant time." There must be something special about the ocean to make it worth four hours of walking for a five-hour visit.

Living as we do, a quick drive away from the seashore, we frequently forget that most Americans don't have such ready access. But during earlier times, living even a few miles inland would make a trip to the beach a difficult process. As Perkins's diary indicates, a walk to the beach took a great deal of effort, even for a couple of very fit farm boys, who most likely walked at a brisk pace. It was not the type of trip a mother might undertake with her hot and sticky little offspring. Older citizens traveled to the beach only if they could get up a "party" and hire a carriage. Middle-aged Hannah Brown headed to the beach in 1852 with a group of church friends: "I went to Hampton Beach in a party. We started from Exeter at seven in the morning, returned at seven in the evening. While there, we amused ourselves in strolling about the beach, and banks, and bathing which I enjoy much. I wish I could go to the saltwater often, my health is much better for it."

She didn't get to the beach that often; however, her diary tells us that she only managed it about once a year. Things improved dramatically later in the century when electric streetcars were installed, linking Exeter with Hampton Beach. By 1909, with very little effort, you could hop on the streetcar in downtown Exeter and ride all the way out to Little Boar's Head in just under an hour for twenty-five cents. Fifteen-year-old Marion Tyler traveled back and forth four times in July and August and had planned more trips that, alas, her father wouldn't allow. Marion's sister, Ruth, was waiting tables at a seaside restaurant that summer. Hampton Beach had become a

A group of bathers show off their fashionable beachwear in Hampton sometime in the 1920s.

tourist attraction and Marion was keen to catch some of the fun. But Ruth was working and the two sisters had to amuse each other with postcards instead. The streetcars transported the mail and a postcard could be sent from Exeter in the morning and arrive at Hampton Beach before lunch. It wasn't quite e-mail, but it was pretty quick.

The streetcars ran through town from 1897 until 1926, eventually linking the entire seacoast of New Hampshire and Amesbury, Massachusetts. During this nearly thirty-year period, trips to the beach became more common and there are still Exeter residents who remember these special trips. Olive Tardiff recalls:

> *The summer trolley was an open car, and the older boys daringly took their places on the steps on the outside, holding onto posts. The younger children (and girls, of course) climbed into the bench-like seats with their mothers. The trolley probably traveled at a speed of about 20 miles and hour, so even the boys hanging on the outside were safe, but every mile was a thrill for us children who seldom had a chance to ride anywhere outside of town.*
>
> *The first excitement was actually seeing the ocean ("I see the sea!" we would chant), the next was stopping in front of the Casino and hurrying up to the long porch on the second floor which must have been reserved by the church for the day. I believe that dressing rooms were available for ten cents, but mothers like mine preferred to save money by holding towels around*

us while we changed into our bathing suits. I can still feel those scratchy woolen suits, especially rough for our tender skins when wet and sandy.

Most of the mothers stayed on the porch, rocking in the old-fashioned chairs and exchanging news and gossip and watching their children at play in the sand. Some ventured into the water with their eager children who mostly jumped and splashed in the frigid water, staying in until almost blue with cold. We built sand castles on the beach and watched with dismay when they were washed away by rising tides. Finally we returned to the porch where picnic baskets were unpacked, and cold lemonade was poured from gallon jugs. Babies were put down for naps, and the rest of us wandered the boardwalk with perhaps only a dime or two to spend.

It was a tired group of children (and mothers, too) that rode home that day, many with sunburned shoulders that itched from damp bathing suits and painful burns on arms and legs, but all with memories of a wonderful day.

HAMPTON BEACH
DISASTER, 1898

July 4 was to be a stellar day at Hampton Beach in 1898. The weather was hot but scores of people from neighboring towns, particularly Exeter, were expected to take the new streetcars for a cool day at the shore. With the recent outbreak of the Spanish-American War, one of the big draws was a new electric stereoscope presentation of "The Sinking of the Maine" at Phineas Beckman's converted roller rink. Frank Nudd took some friends on an excursion trip onboard his sloop. But as the afternoon passed, dark thunderclouds approached from the west, bringing "a black wall of destructiveness and death."

The Exeter Brass Band played a short concert on the porch of the roller rink just prior to the scheduled show. As they finished the last few notes, Beckman noticed the dark clouds approaching and closed the windows just in time for the rain to begin. Instead of a typical rainstorm, the *Exeter News-Letter* reported "ominous thunder clouds overspread the sky, and at nearly half past three one of particularly threatening aspect was seen speeding from the west. Hardly had its furious approach been noted, when it swept the beach and bay, and in a twinkling of an eye claimed nine victims, maimed or wounded scores and wrecked or damaged numerous buildings." Inside the roller rink was a scene of chaos as the roof was torn from the walls. The *Exeter Gazette* reported: "When the building began to crackle and sway, people rushed for the entrance, and scarcely before anyone could get out came the final crash, and the building sunk in like an eggshell and an instant later the air was filled with the shrieks of distracted women and the frenzied calling of men who had missed wife or children." Beckman himself escaped the collapsing building, the walls falling around him, but four people were mortally wounded during the five minutes that the wind raged.

Phineas Beckman's converted roller rink after the storm. The roof was torn from the walls, killing four people.

From the beach, hundreds of people watched helplessly as Captain Nudd's sloop tried to escape the oncoming storm, but the gale blew in too quickly for the small crew. The sloop capsized and five members of the party, including Nudd, were drowned.

What type of storm was this? The National Weather Service was still in its infancy and had no standardized criteria for describing violent weather events. Newspapers referred to the storm as a "cyclone" or "tornado," but none of the eyewitnesses mentioned a tell-tale funnel cloud. Descriptions of the destruction mentioned fallen chimneys, buildings moved off their foundations, barns tossed forward into other buildings, carriages overturned and, like the roller rink, roofs blown off. The roller rink roof was lifted up and rotated on its one remaining corner, falling just in front of the building. The *News-Letter* noted: "had it fallen in, the loss of life must have been enormous. The walls then collapsed with fatal effect." The path of destruction was a half-mile wide, a more typical pattern for an event called a downburst. A downburst is a strong, sudden downdraft from a thunderstorm resulting in an outward burst of damaging winds on or near the ground. Downburst winds can exceed one hundred miles per hour and can do as much damage as a tornado. Downbursts, although rare, are slightly more common in New England than tornados and the two are often confused. The 1898 storm certainly illustrates that either kind of event can be fatal. The 1991 Stratham Hill Park downburst also took lives and left decapitated trees as its calling card. A tornado would have left twisted debris.

The destruction at Hampton Beach increased tourism for a while. Most of the buildings were repaired or cleared away within two weeks—efficiency unknown in our modern insurance-driven recovery process. Most injured victims were discharged from the new Exeter Cottage Hospital within a short time, and the Exeter Brass Band, which had lost one member and received injuries to numerous other players, resumed the summer concert series by August.

HURRICANE OF 1938

New England seems an unlikely place for tropical cyclones, but every once in a great while we are hosts to one of these unwelcome visitors. They happen so infrequently that entire generations can forget the swirling humid winds, torrential rain and flooding waters. Certainly, in 1938 there was no one living who could remember a hurricane reaching the Northeast.

Most tropical storms that hug the Atlantic seaboard veer farther east, following the Gulf Stream. But if the circumstances are just right, if there's a valley of low pressure in just the right location, they can be sucked northwest, and this is exactly what happened in 1938. The hurricane had been brewing for over a week in September, but it was out at sea and there were no land-based tracking stations to report on its development. A few ships had radioed in that it was fierce; still the weather service assumed it would follow the more predictable path and head for the North Atlantic. But this one got away from them and by the time anyone realized the storm was headed for Long Island, it was too late to warn people.

It slammed into Long Island, Connecticut and Rhode Island with such fury that it destroyed weather stations after recording some of the highest wind gusts ever seen in the area. It was most likely a high category 4 or category 5 hurricane when it made its initial landfall. Certainly the storm surge—some damage done to buildings was more than twenty feet above sea level—was characteristic of a category 4 storm. Entire seaside communities were wiped away, sometimes with whole families attached to them. Even today the death toll is uncertain. The Red Cross places the toll at seven hundred killed, thirty-five hundred injured, seventy-five thousand buildings damaged and three thousand boats sunk. A staggering loss in any age.

Historically Speaking

Front Street in Exeter on the morning after the 1938 hurricane.

What most people remember best about this storm was the complete lack of warning. Even today a hurricane's path is difficult to predict. This may be one of the reasons the weather service began naming storms in 1953—they seem almost human-like in their fickle behavior. The seacoast of New Hampshire was caught as off guard as any other area. Although considerably less destructive when it reached Exeter during the early evening of September 21, the hurricane tore through town, playing nine-pins with the stately elm trees in the town center. The *News-Letter* reported two days later that "the town was a shambles Thursday morning." Trees and power lines were down all along Front, High and Lincoln Streets. Crews were out early to make the downtown streets passable, but "it was a new experience for Exeter to have its main residential street blocked by fallen trees, to be cut off for two days from domestic electricity and telephone service, and from street lighting for a longer time, to wake in the morning to the discovery that New York and Chicago could be reached only through the air." There was no loss of life or injury in Exeter, although the paper reported that there were "remarkable escapes of persons and buildings from falling trees." Given the reports of destruction from other parts of New England, Exeter and the surrounding towns breathed a collective sigh of relief.

We would be visited by a hurricane in 1944, but again, we seemed to have escaped most of the devastation. The twin sisters, Carol and Edna, struck within two weeks of one another in 1954, bringing flooding, but improved emergency response systems prevailed. We would do well to remind ourselves to take these occasional visitors quite seriously.

THE ELEPHANT ON
WATER STREET

There are thousands of photographs in the collections of the Exeter Historical Society, but few as interesting as the one of the elephant on Water Street. When Teddie Higgins Smith brought in her Aunt Verna's photo album last year, she commented, "Oh, and here's one of the elephant on Water Street," as though everyone in town knew the story. Well, no one at the Historical Society had heard any particular tale about an elephant, but that didn't mean we couldn't uncover something. We copied the photo and the research began.

The only New England elephant history I've ever come across is the tragic story of the murder of Old Bett in Alfred, Maine. "Old Bett" (or "Big Bett") was owned by Hachaliah Bailey of New York. He'd come across her in a cattle market in New York City sometime after the War of 1812 and purchased her to do farm work. She attracted so much attention on the farm that Bailey decided to take her on the road as a performance artist, which seemed a much better life than pulling stumps in upstate New York. After traveling around the region for a few years, Bailey and Bett found their way to Alfred, Maine, where the unfortunate Bett was shot by a local farmer who believed that he was protecting the townsfolk from breaking the Sabbath to attend frivolous entertainments. Besides, poor people shouldn't be wasting their money to gawk at exotic creatures that ought not to be in this part of the world. Poor Bett lies buried just off Route 4 in Alfred, a reminder of what can happen when a New Englander feels something is out of place.

Sometimes, when Bett's story is told, she is presumed to be the first elephant ever brought to the United States, but that honor falls to "Buffon," an Asian elephant from Bengal brought here by Captian Jacob Crowinshield in 1796. Although we can't know if Bett ever visited Exeter,

Historically Speaking

This photograph—an elephant marching down Water Street past the Merrill Block around 1890—was found in the photograph album of Verna Higgins McGaughey of Exeter. Attempts to positively identify the elephant have proved elusive.

the *Exeter News-Letter* noted, in 1896, that Lyman Greeley owned a poster advertising Buffon's visit to Exeter in 1797:

> *He is so tame that he travels loose, and he never attempted to hurt anyone. A respectable and convenient place is fitted up at James Folsom's, Spring Street, for the reception of those ladies and gentlemen who may be pleased to view the greatest natural curiosity ever presented to the curious, which is to be seen from sunrise to sundown, every day in the week...The elephant having destroyed many papers of consequence, it is recommended to visitors not to come near him with such papers.*

Aunt Verna's elephant, however, was neither of these famous animals. Her photo was taken from a vantage point on Center Street that provides a view of the Merrill Block, built in 1873—long after Bett or Buffon worked in New England. Her elephant was probably part of a traveling circus and its romp down Water Street part of the obligatory circus parade. For quite a while, I was convinced that it was "Bazal," who traveled with Scribner &

Smith's Circus in the 1890s. Bazal made an appearance in town on June 13, 1895. Advertised as "Bazal the Giant Elephant—Largest Ever Captured," I was surprised that I'd never heard of him. A quick note to the Circus Museum in Baraboo, Wisconsin, put me in touch with its curator, Erin Foley. She seriously doubted that Bazal was the "largest ever captured" and seemed to feel he was a she:

> *I don't have any record of this particular elephant, but it does seem unlikely she was the largest ever captured. Many circuses made such claims. Jumbo (the most famous circus elephant) was an average-sized elephant when he toured in 1882–85, and about 11 feet tall.*

Aunt Verna's elephant does appear to be full grown, and good sized, so maybe she was an African and larger than most of the other elephants touring.

So, the photo could be a cross-dressing Bazal, although without any hard evidence to pin down the date of the picture, she still could be any of the many elephants that came to town with the annual arrival of a circus. The tents were pitched in the west end of town behind the shoe factory and although someone, possibly Verna Higgins herself, was quick enough to snap a picture of the elephant, there are no other circus pictures from this period in our collections. And that's a shame, because along with Bazal the Giant Elephant, Scribner & Smith's brought "Lordly Lions, Terrific Tigers, Deadly Jaguars, Monster Pythons, and Weird Monsters of the Forest and Jungle" to town.

The Ghosts that Haunt the Historian

One of the many services we offer at the Exeter Historical Society is assistance with house research. We can't always track down everything about a house, but we are at least familiar with the resources available for researchers. It can be a very thrilling task to trace the owners back through time with directory entries or bits and pieces of information gleaned from newspaper accounts. But at least two or three times a year, I get a client who is interested in more than just a house's history.

"I want to know if anyone died in my house," is the usual inquiry that sends up a red flag.

"How old is your house?" I ask.

"Oh, very old, I think it was built in the 1860s." Since there are far older houses in the Exeter area, we almost consider an 1860 house modern. The hard part is figuring out why this person wants to know about deaths.

"I think I have a ghost and I want to know who it was." Of course! The common belief about ghosts is that they must have had some kind of tragic death and are lingering at the scene because they weren't ready to leave at the time they passed on. The problem is that in an old house—say, anything over one hundred years old—lots of people died. That's where people died—at home. The fact that everyone was born at home, too, never seems to bother anyone. Instead, every weird noise or draft or "creepy feeling" is ascribed to the house ghost.

So I have to find the potential ghost for these folks. Today we tend to consider any death as tragic and often I'm forced to present several possible candidates. It might have been the man who had the sudden heart attack out in the barn, the child who died of diphtheria or the mother who died in childbirth. It could also be the aged widow who slipped away in her sleep still looking for her deceased husband.

The problem with ghosts is that they come all the way from the other side (which can't be easy or everyone would do it) to communicate with us and then they unhelpfully provide scanty information for us to go on. Luckily for us living folk, there are special people who are somehow chosen to communicate with these spirits. Called "mediums," "spiritualists" or even "earth spirit messengers," these people will come to your house and obtain just enough ambiguous, conflicting or nonspecific information to make any story seem possible. I'm not saying that these special people aren't really sensing the ghosts; it's just that the ghosts don't seem to provide us with enough to go on. Why do the ghosts never recall their own last names? They love to tell the mediums their first names—"Charles," "Sarah," "James" or any number of names our early ancestors used over and over, sometimes within a single generation—but they have never said, "Oh, and my surname was Gilman and I lived in the 1700s." It would be so helpful if they would.

I also wish mediums had a better grasp of history. Telling me that a ghost was killed "during the war" gives me nothing to go on. For crying out loud, please ask the ghost which war. Once I was presented with a ghost named Charles who said he received bad news in the '40s and was wearing a blue shirt and a cap. Unfortunately, the farm he was associated with had been in cultivation since the 1690s and Charles might have lived in the 1740s, 1840s or 1940s. I did find a Charles related to the family, but he was living in Boston when he got his bad news. I don't know why he would be hanging around his father's farm a century later. The medium also missed the tortured souls of thousands of cattle who stopped on the land on their way to the Brighton Cattle market. I would have thought that anyone who could talk to boulders would pick up on all those angry cows.

I wish I were one of the special people who could talk to ghosts. I have a lot of questions for anyone who lived in the past. I might even be able to identify the period the ghost lived in by looking a bit more closely at its clothes. What kind of cap? A tricorn? And I'm reasonably convinced my follow-up questions during the usual ghostly interview might steer things in the right direction.

My own house is over 230 years old. One of the people who died there was Ella Gilman Templeton—probably in the bedroom where I sleep every night. Never once has she come back to have a chat with me. I really wish she would. She and her husband, John Templeton (who died next door in his son's house), ran the *Exeter News-Letter* for over 50 years. It would be great to have her as a hot line to the *News-Letter*'s past. Would she find it as weird as I do that I sit composing pieces for the *News-Letter* in her house, just as she and her husband did 100 years ago? Would she approve of our recent kitchen renovation? And why, oh why, did she choose that awful wallpaper in the old dining room? Maybe John was colorblind. I'd like to know.

ACKNOWLEDGEMENTS

In the course of my work in the field of history, I've come to realize that the greatest historical resource we have is people. Exeter is lucky to have a population of senior residents who are more than willing to contribute their knowledge to our record. It is one thing to read about events; it is quite another to chat with someone who actually remembers what the weather was like that day. I think I know more people over the age of ninety than most. I am indebted particularly to Thelma Barlow, Olive Tardiff and William Gustin for their broad knowledge and great wisdom. I also appreciate their wit. Bill volunteered at the Exeter Historical Society for ten years, until he decided to retire from his retirement at the youthful age of ninety-two. He read and edited many of the pieces in this book. Thelma and Olive, also over ninety, would until recently go out to lunch together on Saturdays and only order ice cream. Once you're over ninety, Thelma explained, you can do that.

My loyal coworker, Laura Martin Gowing, tolerates my biweekly frenzy when trying to get a column in before deadline. I've interrupted her work on more occasions than I'd like to count to have her read all or parts of an almost-incoherent piece. She is always gracious and, thankfully, very honest in her assessment of my mangled prose. I have to both thank her and publicly apologize for the often-heated debates we have concerning punctuation.

My brother, Tony Rimkunas, an actual English major, was willing to read through nearly ninety columns to help choose the few included in this book. I was astonished at his choices—these were like my children and he willingly sent some off to the salt mines. However, his eye is good and he corrected a number of grammar atrocities that would have proved quite embarrassing. I put "The Ghosts that Haunt the Historian" back in even though there was no photo to go with it and Tony said it was a rant that had no historical merit. I am the older sister, after all.

Acknowledgements

Joe McCarthy, of Exeter, wrote the line "George Washington stepped here." I stole it. I admit it freely.

My husband, Mike, and our daughters, Nelly and Alice, have been supportive even if the only way I can get them to read my work is to clip it out of the newspaper and leave it in the bathroom. They have provided numerous ideas for columns and have had to listen to me telling all these wild stories during supper. Nelly's friend, Valerie Goeman, once challenged me to write something with the word "antidisestablishmentarianism" in it. I almost made it. Alice, when about three years old, once summed up my entire career as: "Mommy works with dead people."

And, of course, Nancy Merrill, who no longer recognizes me when we encounter one another face to face. I, however, encounter Nancy almost daily at the Exeter Historical Society. Her handwriting, her research, her voice and her warmth are still here.

About the Author

Barbara Rimkunas grew up in Falmouth, Maine. She attended and taught at Catherine McAuley High School in Portland. She has a BA and MA in history from the Universities of Maine and New Hampshire, respectively, which makes the college hockey season somewhat tense.

She worked as an archaeologist during the 1984 season at Fort Pentagoet in Castine, Maine. She also spent over six years working in patient registration in the emergency department at Exeter Hospital while in graduate school, which trained her to type very quickly while under great pressure—a skill rarely required at the Exeter Historical Society.

Budd Perry Photograph

She writes a biweekly column called *Historically Speaking* for the *Exeter News-Letter*.

She is currently curator at the Exeter Historical Society, where she can often be found scurrying around the darkened archives on absolutely breathtaking summer days, pale and chilled like a naked mole rat.

Visit us at
www.historypress.net